3D Character Rigging in Blender

Bring your characters to life through rigging and make them animation-ready

Jaime Kelly

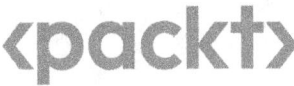

3D Character Rigging in Blender

Copyright © 2024 Packt Publishing

Group Product Manager: Rohit Rajkumar

Publishing Product Manager: Vaideeshwari Muralikrishnan

Book Project Manager: Aishwarya Mohan

Senior Editor: Aamir Ahmed and Nathanya Dias

Technical Editor: Simran Haresh Udasi

Copy Editor: Safis Editing

Indexer: Manju Arasan

Production Designer: Prashant Ghare

DevRel Marketing Coordinators: Anamika Singh and Nivedita Pandey

First published: April 2024

Production reference: 1010324

Published by Packt Publishing Ltd.

Grosvenor House

11 St Paul's Square

Birmingham

B3 1RB, UK

ISBN: 978-1-80323-880-7

www.packtpub.com

Contributors

About the author

Jaime Kelly is a freelance artist with over five years of experience with works in animation, rigging, and 3D design. He has worked within all manners of industries, including product promotion materials, animated media such as animated breakdowns of systems in training material, and, of course, 3D rigging for pre-rendered and real-time media.

To the creators, contributors, and supporters of Blender – thank you for making the most powerful and versatile 3D software ever, free of use for everyone.

About the reviewers

Buhonero75 is a normal person like anyone, with dreams like anyone. He is a 3D modeler, animator, and video game creator, and the models he makes always challenge people's criteria a little. He makes the models based on his creativity or whatever he wants. He believes that the internet needs a change, and he is someone who opposes the restrictions of this time. The best thing you can do is do what you want without letting anyone stop you.

Mohamed Essam El Deen Farouk is a passionate and creative 3D artist who loves to bring his imagination to life. He has six years of experience in the 3D industry, working with various tools and software such as Blender 3D, Substance 3D Painter, and Unreal Engine. He specializes in modeling, rigging, and texturing characters and creatures for games.

He is a 3D artist/rigger at Game Art Brain GmbH, an outsourcing studio for stylized 2D and 3D game art. He was also one of the technical reviewers who worked on the book *Sculpting the Blender Way*. He is always eager to learn new skills and techniques, challenging himself with different and complex projects. He enjoys collaborating with other artists and developers and sharing his knowledge and feedback.

Benon Nyabuto is a seasoned Blender character animator with four-plus years in the industry. His expertise lies in the intricacies of rigging and animation processes, cultivated through learning from industry luminaries such as Pierrick Picaut, Chester Sampson, and Richard Shilling. Renowned for his innovative rigging and animation systems, Benon brings a unique flair to captivate audiences. Notable projects in his portfolio include *Plant vs Frenemies*, *Wasoko Ad*, *Copia Ad*, and *Dance Girl*. Connect with him on LinkedIn as *Benon Nyabuto* or follow his creative journey on social media (@ animator_benny).

Table of Contents

Part 2: Rigging

Part 3: Advanced Techniques

6

7

8

Preface

In this book, *3D Character Rigging in Blender*, we will start with an unrigged character mesh and end with an effective tool for animators to bring life to an otherwise static mesh, going from the basics of Blender to advanced rigging techniques. Starting with a human figure and placing all the bones needed for complete and convincing motion, we will learn handy tips and cover the reasoning behind many of the actions taken to make you able to eventually make your own decisions in your work.

Who this book is for

Anyone with or without experience in Blender who wishes to learn the foundations of character rigging and produce reliable, clean rigs for animation will benefit from this book. No background in computer graphics is required but any experience in Blender will allow you to focus on the rigging and less on learning the software (which is also taught throughout this book). This book is primarily aimed at beginners.

What this book covers

Chapter 1, Introduction to Rigs and Terminologies, serves to introduce you to both Blender and the basics of rigs.

Chapter 2, Starting with Bones, sees us creating and editing bones while becoming familiar with Blender.

Chapter 3, Using Weighting Tools to Give Life to a Mesh, shows how we tie meshes to bones with weight painting.

Chapter 4, Beginning the Rigging Process, is where we start work on the centerpiece of the book by placing bones.

Chapter 5, Getting Started with Weight Painting, continues the trajectory from *Chapter 4* with an examination of weight-painting meshes to bones.

Chapter 6, Using IK and Rig Controls, covers the automatic controls available in Blender.

Chapter 7, Getting Started with Shape Keys, offers a light introduction to shape keys, taking you from creating shape keys to using drivers.

Chapter 8, Beyond the Basics, offers a collection of more advanced techniques to provide paths for further improvement of your skills in more advanced applications.

To get the most out of this book

You will need to install Blender. The exercises in this book are composed with Blender 3.2 in mind. Blender is easily downloadable from the official Blender website at `https://www.blender.org/` and is supported by all major platforms.

You will also need to download the resources provided: `https://github.com/PacktPublishing/3D-Character-Rigging-in-Blender`.

Software/hardware covered in the book	Operating system requirements
Blender	Windows, macOS, or Linux

Screenshots are included throughout this book, some of them with small UI elements. While all important areas are marked and annotated, reading a digital copy to zoom in on the images might help.

Download the example code files

You can download the example files for this book from GitHub at `https://github.com/PacktPublishing/3D-Character-Rigging-in-Blender`.

If there's an update to the resources provided, it will be updated in the GitHub repository.

We also have other bundles from our rich catalog of books and videos available at `https://github.com/PacktPublishing/`. Check them out!

Conventions used

There are several text conventions used throughout this book.

Highlighted text: Indicates physical keys you should press in the written order, with the mouse in the correct area (shortcut keys are contextual to cursor location).

Here is an example: "They will also still be parented to the arm, which will cause a dependency loop, so make sure you clear the parent with *Alt + P* ."

Bold: Indicates a new term, an important word, or words that you see onscreen. For instance, words in menus or dialog boxes appear in **bold**. Here is an example: "To add a new shape key, navigate to **Object data properties | Shape keys** and click the **Plus** button." In this example, each successive action is a menu selection that leads to the next one.

> **Tips or important notes**
> Appear like this.

Get in touch

Feedback from our readers is always welcome.

General feedback: If you have questions about any aspect of this book, email us at customercare@ packtpub.com and mention the book title in the subject of your message.

Errata: Although we have taken every care to ensure the accuracy of our content, mistakes do happen. If you have found a mistake in this book, we would be grateful if you would report this to us. Please visit www.packtpub.com/support/errata and fill in the form.

Piracy: If you come across any illegal copies of our works in any form on the internet, we would be grateful if you would provide us with the location address or website name. Please contact us at copyright@packt.com with a link to the material.

If you are interested in becoming an author: If there is a topic that you have expertise in and you are interested in either writing or contributing to a book, please visit authors.packtpub.com.

Share Your Thoughts

Once you've read *3D Character Rigging in Blender*, we'd love to hear your thoughts! Scan the QR code below to go straight to the Amazon review page for this book and share your feedback.

https://packt.link/r/1-803-23880-1

Your review is important to us and the tech community and will help us make sure we're delivering excellent quality content.

Download a free PDF copy of this book

Thanks for purchasing this book!

Do you like to read on the go but are unable to carry your print books everywhere?

Is your eBook purchase not compatible with the device of your choice?

Don't worry, now with every Packt book you get a DRM-free PDF version of that book at no cost.

Read anywhere, any place, on any device. Search, copy, and paste code from your favorite technical books directly into your application.

The perks don't stop there, you can get exclusive access to discounts, newsletters, and great free content in your inbox daily

Follow these simple steps to get the benefits:

1. Scan the QR code or visit the link below

https://packt.link/free-ebook/978-1-80323-880-7

2. Submit your proof of purchase

3. That's it! We'll send your free PDF and other benefits to your email directly

Part 1:
An Introduction

In the first part of this book, we will look at setting up Blender and familiarize ourselves with both Blender and the common terminology used within both Blender and rigging. This part will also overlap with *Part 2*, featuring more technical work.

This part has the following chapters:

- *Chapter 1, Introduction to Rigs and Terminologies*
- *Chapter 2, Starting with Bones*

1

Introduction to Rigs and Terminologies

This book will offer detailed instructions to help you build your own rigs using Blender, a free and open source 3D software used by many worldwide to produce stunning visuals, assets, and stories. You will progress from adding bones to an empty scene and learning how to weight paint to rigging a humanoid character in Blender, while learning all the necessary buttons for rigging and success-boosting tips. You will then move on to implementing advanced features such as drivers, constraints, and custom handles, all of which will be expected of a professional rig. By the end of this book, you will have the ability to create rigs of all shapes and sizes, compatible with the pipelines of many teams and studios.

In this first chapter, we will start by understanding the basic terminologies that will be used throughout this book and are necessary to follow along. We will start with the anatomy of bones and how they work together to produce rigs. Then, we will install Blender, learn the key aspects of its UI, and get familiar with its shortcuts.

In this chapter, we will cover the following topics:

- Terminology – understanding the anatomy of a bone

- Understanding the structure of a rig

- Starting with Blender

By the end of this chapter, you will be able to install Blender and know what rigs are used for and the individual components that make them up.

The following figure shows a collection of rigged 3D characters; take a quick look if you are not already familiar with what 3D rigs look like:

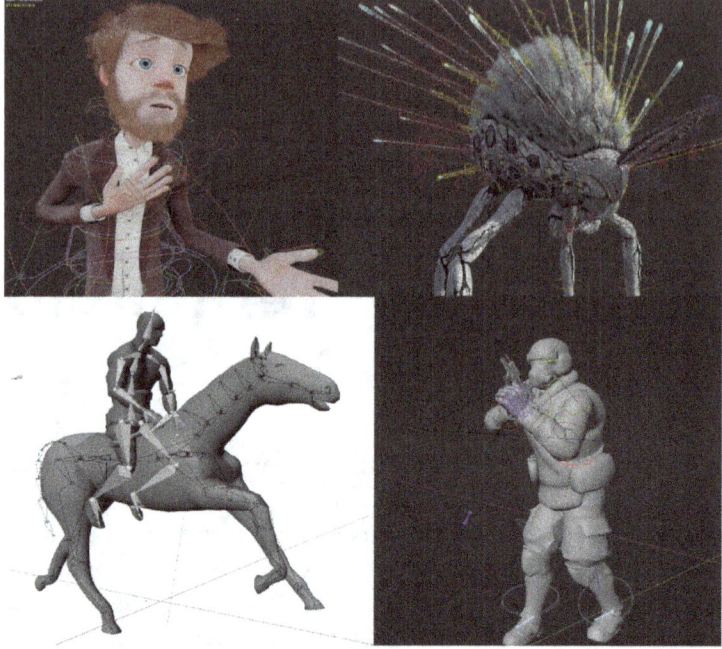

Figure 1.1 – Example rigs (source – the top-left and top-right images were taken from Blender Studio)

Technical requirements

Anything later than the following will be able to run Blender:

Operating system: Windows 8.1+, macOS 10.13+, or Linux

I recommend you use a system with 8 GB of system memory and at least a modern dual-core processor. Blender is exceptionally easy to run; the tasks you will tackle in this book will pose no more than a light workload for any computer built within the last five years.

You can find out more on the official Blender website: https://www.Blender.org/download/requirements/.

Terminology – understanding the anatomy of a bone

We need to start somewhere, so let's get ourselves acquainted with the basics of bones and rigs!

Figure 1.2 shows a single bone, which is the basic building block of any rig:

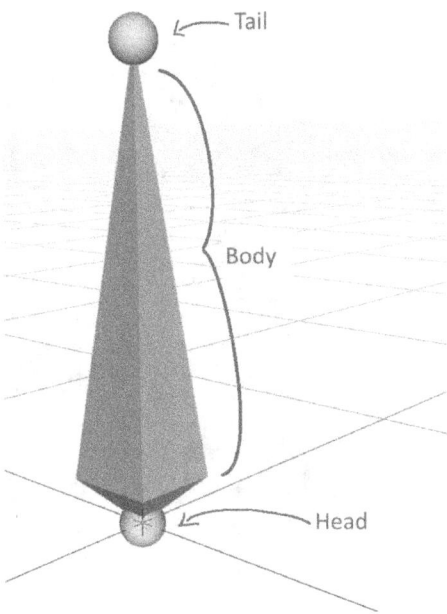

Figure 1.2 – A single bone

Bones on their own are remarkably simple; they consist of a **Head**, a **Tail**, and a **Body**. Heads and tails are pretty confusing, as they are the opposite of what you might think. The head is at the bottom and the tail is at the top. If you struggle to remember, just think about how for most animals with a tail, it's smaller than their head.

Bones typically work in a **hierarchy**, going head to tail to form **chains**, with the first bone being at the top of the hierarchy. All bones after the first bone within the same chain will be shown under it in the **Outliner** window. When multiple chains are part of a single rig, there will be a selected master bone, a **root** bone; typically, this has authority over all the other bones in the rig. This is important to note when we move on to **posing** the bone in the *Using Pose Mode* section in *Chapter 2*.

The head and tail of the bone should be thought of as pivot joints for other bones (much like our own bones). The purpose of the body in Blender is to separate the head and tail.

Blender has a few built-in methods to display bones. *Figure 1.2* was **octahedral**. Pictured in the following figure are all the different display methods. The display method does not alter the function of the bones in any way; it alters their appearance and nothing else.

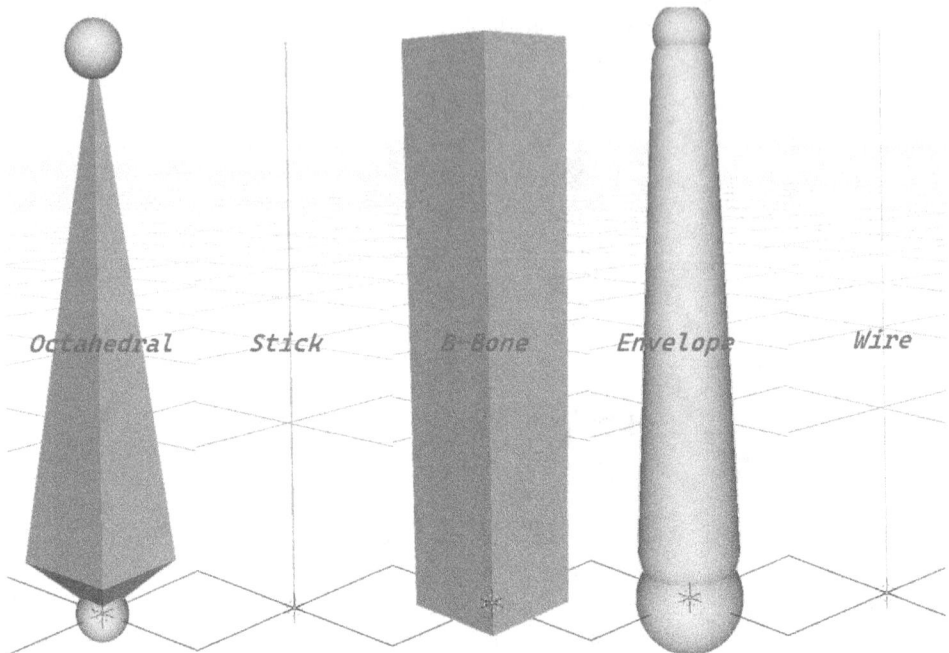

Figure 1.3 – Bone display modes

That covers bones! They really are that simple; their complexity comes with how they exist within Blender's 3D space and interact with other bones and the mesh around them.

Next, we will cover the three bone transforms – **scale**, **location**, and **rotation**. However, these transforms apply to almost anything in Blender.

Bone transforms

As with any object in Blender, bones have transform properties too; pictured in *Figure 1.3* are the axes for this bone. They have scale, location, and rotation.

One thing to note is that there are different transform orientations within Blender; unless stated otherwise, we will refer to **global** space.

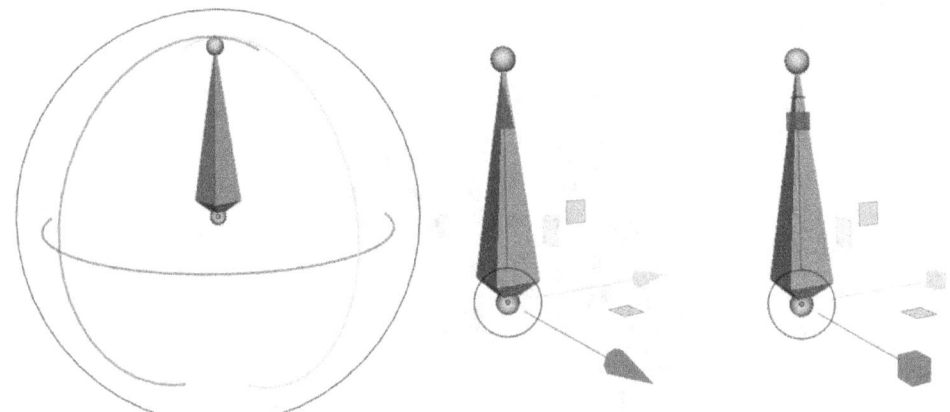

Figure 1.4 – The rotation, location, and scale transforms on a bone

Let's look at the **transform** properties in detail:

- **Rotation**: Commonly referred to as bone roll, this is the Z axis points from the tail to the head. Rotating the Y axis will spin the bone and, along with that, the X and Z axes. It's important you remember this for later on, as the orientation of X and Z will affect how you interact with and pose bones and how certain constraints work. The Z axis is the normal; when we change where it points, it spins the bone. This is also referred to as the **bone** roll. This will be briefly covered when we come to create a rig for ourselves.

- **Location**: This is the same for bones as it is for anything else in Blender; it defines where in the world the bone is, just like any other use for the word *location*. X is shown in red, Y is shown in green, and Z is shown in blue. Location isn't too important for now, but the axes shown in *Figure 1.4* also apply to any location transforms on any object.

- **Scale**: This is the bone's physical size. Bones can only be scaled on the Z axis in Edit Mode, although you will most likely not scale bones outside of Edit Mode. You can scale in Pose Mode to get some cool animation styles, but you most definitely shouldn't scale in Object Mode! Scaling in Object Mode is the quickest way to start an hour-long bug-squashing quest.

Having covered the anatomy of the bone (head, body, and tail) and 3D transforms (rotate, scale, and location), we can now cover the surface of rigs by introducing ourselves to common components and points of interest.

Understanding the structure of a rig

In this section, we will introduce you to rigs, the core of this book. This will touch on topics such as IK and FK, handles, and shapes, and then we will move on to using Blender and its controls to make our first rig. Take a look at *Figure 1.5*; it's a simple rig made up of bones.

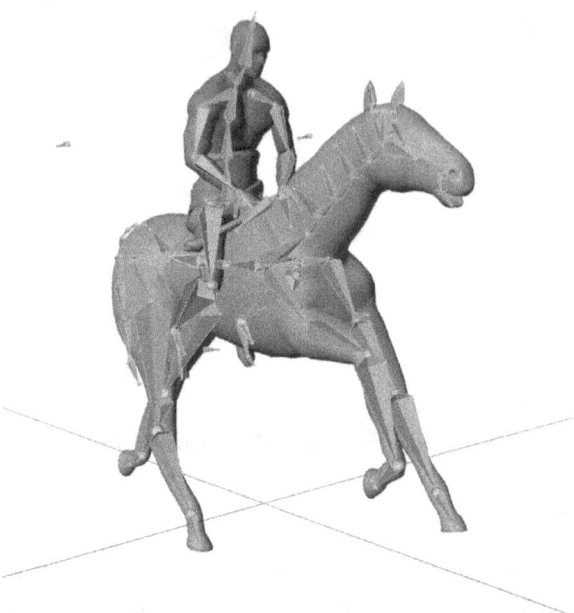

Figure 1.5 – A rigged human atop a rigged horse

Some points of interest in this rig are as follows:

- **Tails flow into heads**: Bones never meet tail to tail or head to head.

- **Some bones have different colors**: This is Blender's default way to show which bones have special **properties**, **relationships**, or **constraints**. You don't need to worry about this for now; it's just nice to know that these colors highlight bones with significance.

- **Floating bones**: Up to now, I have maintained the idea that bones are used to deform a mesh; however, that isn't always true. Sometimes, you will find bones with a different purpose. In *Figure 1.5*, they are used to control the position of any held items that we need to animate but are **not an attached part of the character**. Other uses include inputs for bone drivers and IK controls. I'll introduce you to both drivers and IK later on.

Now that we understand how bones fit inside a rig and their many surprising purposes, it is time to get started with Blender.

Starting with Blender

Before we begin with anything practical, we will need to set up Blender. It's relatively simple to do; it installs just like any other program, and we will not change any of its default settings right now.

Setting up Blender

Before proceeding, we must ensure we're all starting on the same page. In this book, we will use *Blender 3.2.2*. You can go ahead and download it from the official Blender website: `https://www.Blender.org`. Make sure you meet the minimum requirements to run Blender. Anything that can browse the web will probably be able to run Blender.

To set up Blender, follow these steps:

1. Go to the official Blender website (`https://www.Blender.org`) and download it. The version number usually doesn't matter, but if you download *Blender 3.2.2*, you can make sure everything works as this book is written with that in mind.

2. Install Blender by running the `Blender-x.x.x-windows-x64.msi` file and follow the onscreen instructions: `https://www.Blender.org/`.

> **Important note**
>
> For macOS, you will need to choose between **Apple silicon** or **Intel** for the installer; the only way to know whether you're using an Intel Mac or an Apple silicon Mac is by using the **About This Mac** feature. Linux is a standard package just like any other app and can be obtained at the Snap Store.

3. Once Blender is installed, you should make sure you use the default settings; you can load these by going to **File | Defaults | Load Factory Settings**:

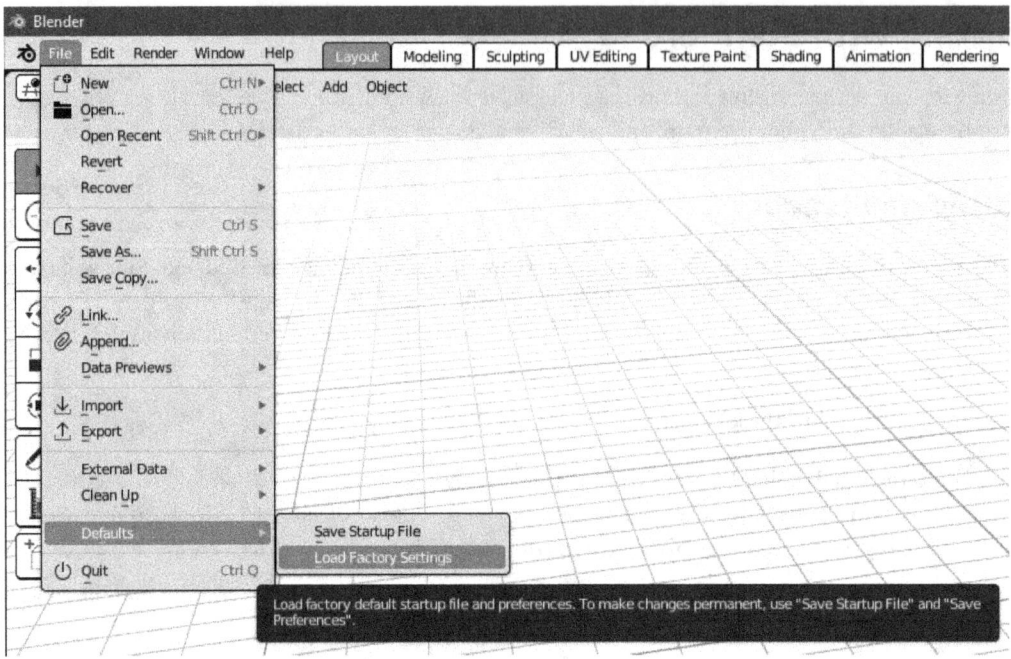

Figure 1.6 – The Load Factory Settings option

> **Important note**
>
> Factory settings are not permanent unless you save the startup file.

4. If you have a fresh installation and haven't touched anything, then you should be ready to go! Open up Blender and create an empty scene by hitting *A* to select all and pressing the *Del* key to delete everything in the 3D scene. Don't worry – we don't need these items for what we're doing. Your scene should look like this:

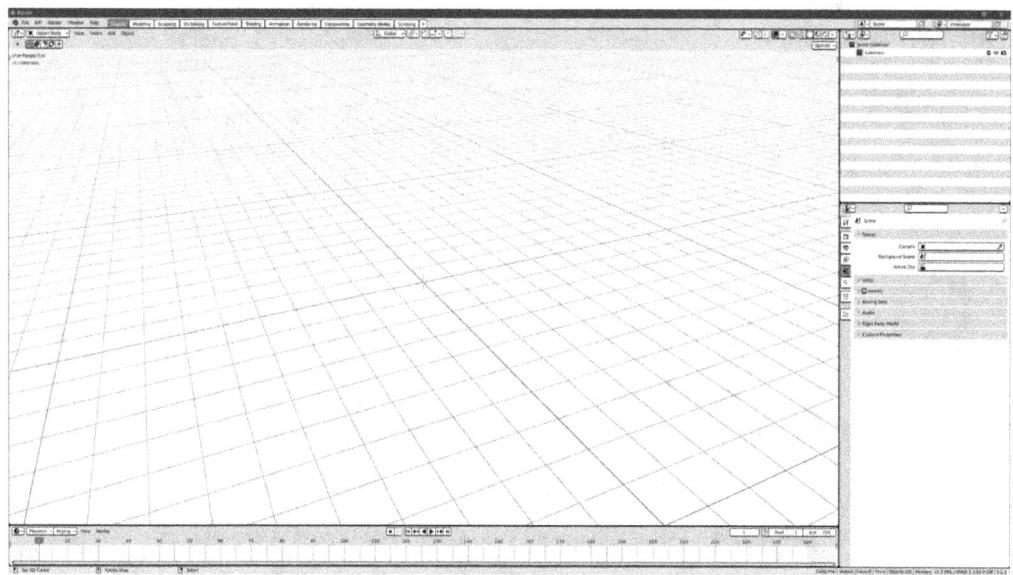

Figure 1.7 – An overview of an empty scene

5. Your Blender scene may look different from mine; I have a light theme applied for ease of reading. However, that should be the only difference. All UI elements should be in the same place; you can modify any part of the UI and save it so that the next time you launch Blender, you can start in a workspace that is more comfortable for you. Simply head to **File | Defaults | Save Startup File**.

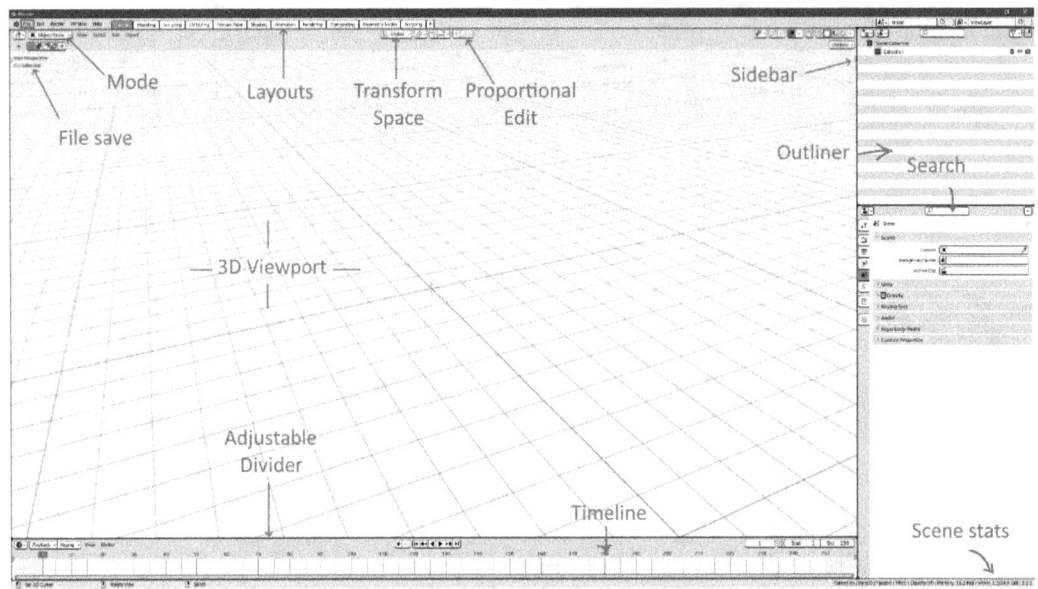

Figure 1.8 – The elements of the UI labeled

Figure 1.8 shows elements of the default UI layout; the important parts will be discussed in greater detail when necessary. However, you can still use this figure to help with navigating.

Summary

After reading this chapter, you should now have a good idea of what bones and rigs look like and how they can translate (move) and transform (scale).

We then moved on to installing Blender from the official website. It's important you only install trusted software, as there are a fair number of websites that offer Blender; however, you will find all of them (apart from the official website) contain malware. Finally, we finished the chapter by showing a handy screenshot of some labeled UI elements; again, this isn't too important currently because we will cover important UI elements when necessary.

This was a short chapter just to get you up to speed with some basic terminology and ideas about rigging. It's pretty much all there is for the hands-off theory that we will cover; the rest of the book will be an all-practical approach to learning rigging in Blender. If you're not sure about anything we have covered, you don't need to worry – it'll become clearer with time. Anything important will be repeated or explained in further detail when necessary.

In the next chapter, we will start our first practical task – placing bones inside objects to bring life to a mesh while learning many of the vital controls used in Blender, from adjusting your view to adding and editing objects in a scene.

2
Starting with Bones

In the previous chapter, we became familiar with the building blocks of rigs and how bones work together to form a rig, and we installed Blender.

In this chapter, we will start with adding objects to the empty scene and learn how to select objects. We will then move on to manipulate the viewport and navigate the 3D space around our work. We will then learn how to add an armature, which is also known as the container for bones (the *rig*). After that, we will learn how to edit this armature to add more bones and form a chain. Finally, we will see how to use different modes, such as **EDIT** and **POSE**, to perform more complex actions on selected objects, such as rotating bones in **POSE** mode.

In this chapter, we will cover the following topics:

- Adding objects to the scene
- Placing our first bones
- Using Pose Mode

By the end of this chapter, you will be able to add objects to a scene. You will have a good understanding of transformations for objects and how to use them, along with understanding views and how to change your view for better visibility of your work. We will close out by looking at adding bones in edit mode and posing bones in pose mode. This will set you up for *Chapter 3*.

Adding objects to the scene

We can't do much with an empty scene, so let's fix that by adding an object to the scene.

1. An object can be anything from mesh and bone to particles and curves. We will be adding an armature object for now. This information should stick with you, and you should have no problem with adding a plethora of objects from the **Add object** dropdown:

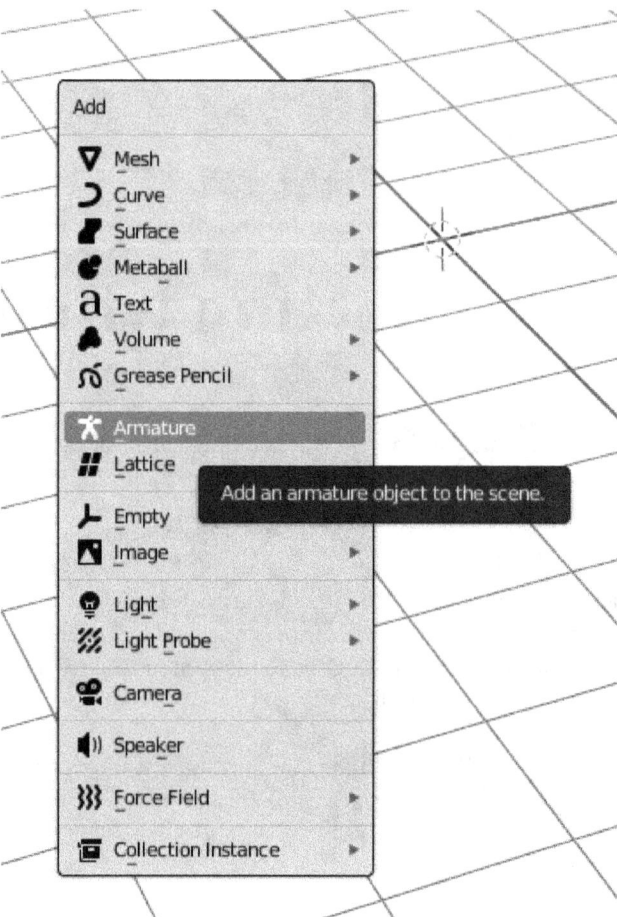

Figure 2.1 – Add menu for adding objects to the scene

Important note

Keyboard shortcuts are context-based depending on where your mouse is within Blender. Placing your mouse inside the 3D viewport and pressing *Shift* + *A* will let you add objects. That's very different from, say, pressing *Shift* + *A* inside the Shader Editor, which would let you add shader nodes. So, be mindful of where your mouse is.

Time for us to begin, starting with the basics and working our way up. Read carefully as this can get very overwhelming for new Blender users.

2. Go ahead and place an armature. This is just an object for the bones to be under. Do this by pressing *Shift + A* while your mouse is inside the **3D** viewport (where the 3D grid with the axes lines is), then moving down the add object popup to **Armature**. If you see a single bone appear, then congratulations, you have your first bone!

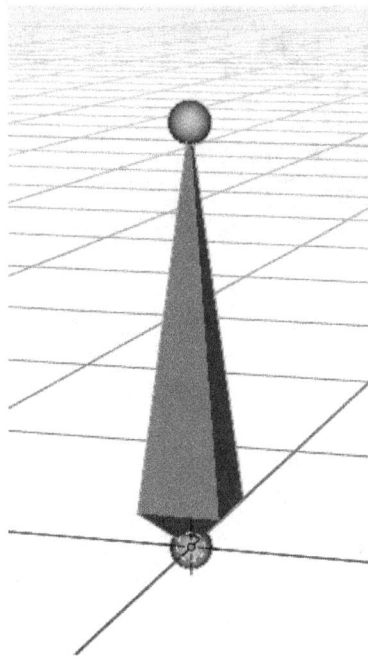

Figure 2.2 – Armatures come with a single bone already made for us

3. The next step is to move into **Edit** mode; we are currently in **Object** mode.

4. Press **Tab** to move between **Object** and **Edit** Mode. You will see some elements of the UI change when you do this, most notably this dropdown in the top left:

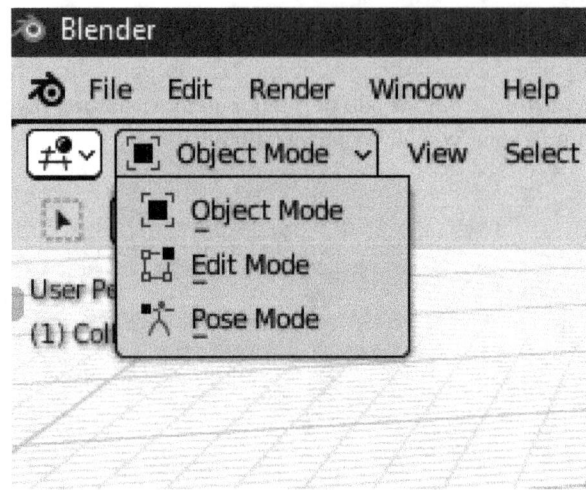

Figure 2.3 – Mode dropdown

5. We need this dropdown to read **Edit Mode** to continue, which we can do by either pressing *Tab* or clicking on the dropdown (*Tab* is faster).

    Object Mode allows us to perform more complex actions on any selected object. Depending on what object we have selected, we will be offered different pose modes.

    This applies to most objects. Using **Edit Mode** on a mesh will let you edit the individual vertices. **Edit Mode** for an irradiance volume is different again, letting you change its dimensions. If you enter **Edit Mode** and get an unexpected result, make sure you have selected the correct object.

An armature is an object with its own unique modes. Once we go into Edit Mode, we can access the bones inside the armature with **Pose Mode**. We will cover how to select objects next. This is another very important skill and it shouldn't be too hard to grasp.

Selecting objects

After adding multiple objects, we need to be able to select any chosen object to interact with it. In this section, we're going to learn how to do just that.

We can select objects in many different ways. Here are a couple:

- Pressing *A* to select, then *A* again to deselect *all* objects in the scene (*Alt* + *A* can also deselect)
- Using a **left mouse click (LMB)** to select what's under our mouse

We will discuss more selection methods as and when needed.

Now that we are in **Edit** mode, you can go ahead and click on the head, body, and tail. When selecting anything in Blender, it will have an orange outline to show your selection. In the images, however, you will sometimes notice I have different colors. This is just because my Blender theme is modified to make it easier for you to see what I'm doing.

Make sure you are comfortable with selecting items in Blender. You're going to be doing it *a lot*.

> **Quick shortcuts**
>
> *Shift + A*: **Add Object**, *Tab*: **Object Mode**, *Del*: **Delete**, *A*: **Select/Deselect**

So, we added a bone to our empty scene, making sure our mouse was in the correct place. We also entered Edit mode to allow us to edit our armature and get comfortable with selecting items in Blender.

Next, before we turn this bone into a multi-bone armature, we need to learn how to use the camera.

Adjusting our view

Adjusting your view usually uses the **middle mouse button** (**MMB**), which is the scroll wheel when it's clicked. The following actions will involve the MMB to move the view around our work in 3D, another very important skill. If you have little experience in 3D applications, then this might be difficult to grasp, but you will get the hang of it with time.

Focus

Every view action, such as panning and zooming, is done using a focal point.

To set a focal point, do the following:

1. Select an object.
2. Press . on the number pad.

You'll notice your viewport focuses on the selected object. However, at this point, your object is in the middle of the scene, and so the view (already focused on the middle) will not change.

Pan

Pan is very important; it's how we can easily view all angles of our focused object. Pan can be described as spinning a globe to instantly view it from any direction. It's another exceptionally important feature, so you'll need to get used to it.

It's the simplest control to use. Simply click your scroll wheel (this button is also called the MMB) and drag your mouse.

If we have an object selected, this will orbit the selected object, which is very handy.

Zoom

Using zoom, we can get a closer view of our work or a broader look at a large amount of work. Zoom is on the scroll wheel, go ahead and test this. You will notice that your view zooms in and out from the middle. We can change the focal point of our zoom by selecting an object to focus on. Press **.** on the number pad to focus your view on the selected object. With this, you can easily change your focus.

Lateral movement

Much like how you can use grabbing and dragging actions in Google Maps, you can do these things in Blender too:

1.   Pan with *Shift* + middle mouse button.
2.   Orbit with middle mouse button.
3.   Zoom with scroll wheel.
4.   Focus a selected object with numpad .
5.   Click your scroll wheel, or MMB, and drag your mouse around.

Figure 2.4 provides a handy quick reference:

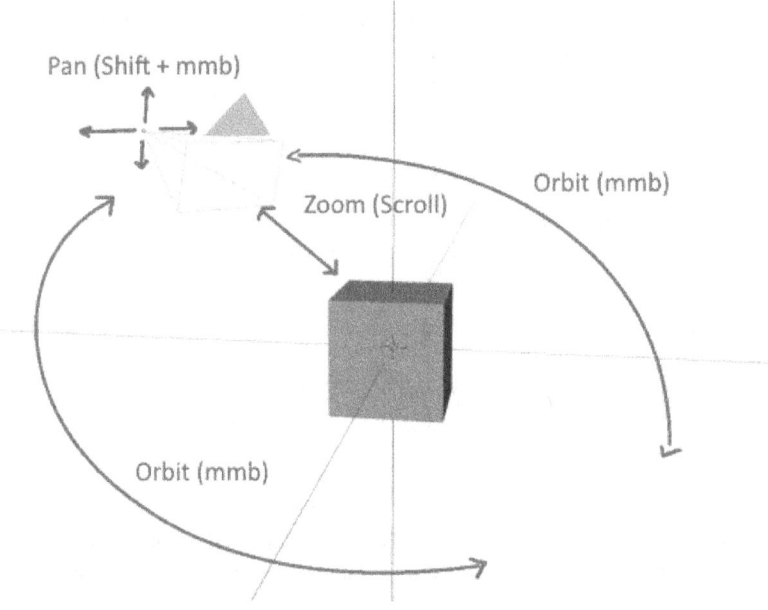

Figure 2.4 – View controls recap

Next. let's look at the orthographic view.

Orthographic view

This is more of a display mode than a way to move our view. It's a complex topic to explain, so I will use this figure as a reference:

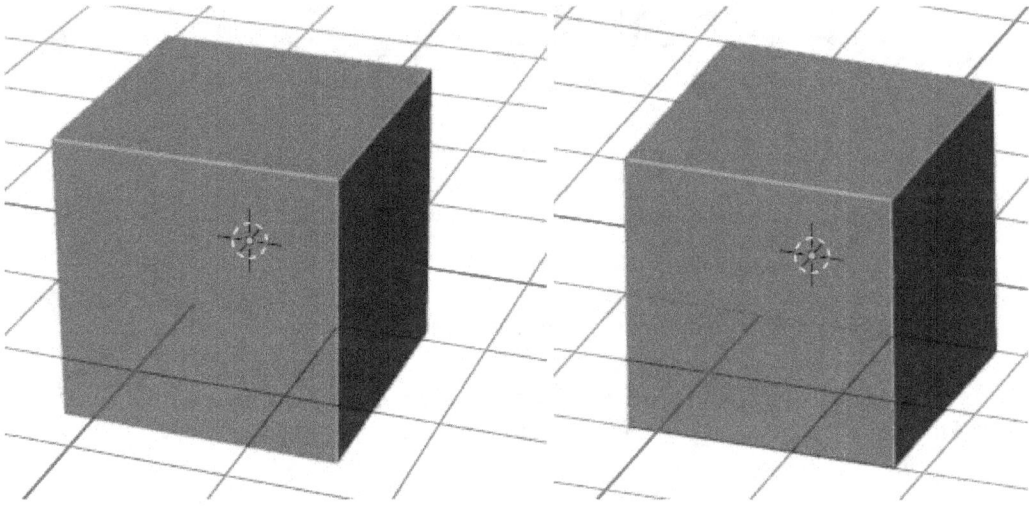

Figure 2.5 – Perspective left, orthographic right

Orthographic view (the right-hand cube) is a means of representing three-dimensional objects in two dimensions. We don't need to understand its complexity to appreciate its usefulness. Just know it helps align things without any 3D perspective issues.

Pressing *5* on the keypad will enter an orthographic view from where the camera is currently: not useful.

Elevation views are what we want. The front, back, and sides in orthographic view. To enter one of these views, hold the MMB and *Alt*, then flick the mouse in any direction. It's like panning with the MMB alone but instead of a smooth orbit, you snap to preset views.

You will want to get comfortable with this as it's handy for aligning elements later on. Once you have entered an orthographic view, it will be shown in the top left, like so:

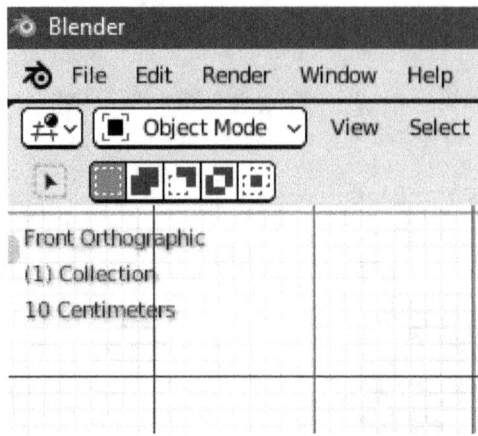

Figure 2.6 – Text showing current view information

If you're struggling to use the MMB, then you can use the *7*, *9*, *1*, and *3* keys on your number pad. Keep flicking around to cycle through the views until you have front orthographic view, then we're ready to continue.

We use this mode to align objects in a more calculated and precise manner than what we could achieve in the orbit view.

> **Quick shortcuts**
>
> Focus: . (number pad), zoom: scroll wheel, Pan: MMB, lateral: MMB + *Shift*, orthographic sides: *Alt* + MMB

So, by now, we should know how to place objects with *Shift* + *A*, which displays the **Add** object menu and allows us to select objects. You should also be getting comfortable with controlling your view in the 3D viewport, which is important.

We'll now move on to adding and editing bones in edit mode to create chains, as well as understanding more about bone normals and translations.

Placing our first bones

We started this chapter by using the **Add** object menu to add an armature. With our armature object in the scene, we can go ahead and start adding bones. Make sure you are in **Edit Mode** for this and in **Front Orthographic** view. Then, go ahead and follow these steps:

1. Have the tail selected and input the following: $E \mid Z$, then move the mouse up and notice a new bone appearing out from our first bone. Pressing the LMB will confirm this action with any translation we have made. Pressing the **right mouse button** (**RMB**) will confirm the extrude but cancel any transforms we have made.

2. The E key in this case is for **Extrude**. The Z key was to select the Z axis as we just want the bone to be extruded straight up. If you want to extrude along any other axis, then press the corresponding key out of X, Y, and Z. You can hold *Shift* and then press a key to select the inverse axis (pressing *Shift* + Z will select X and Y but exclude Z).

Repeat this for a total of three bones. You should have something like this:

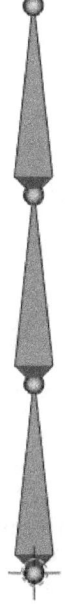

Figure 2.7 – Bone chain

3. Go ahead and select the body of the first bone and press *Shift + D* to duplicate. You should have entered grab automatically after duplicating, so place this bone on the left side to start the next chain of bones. You can see where I placed mine in *Figure 2.8*:

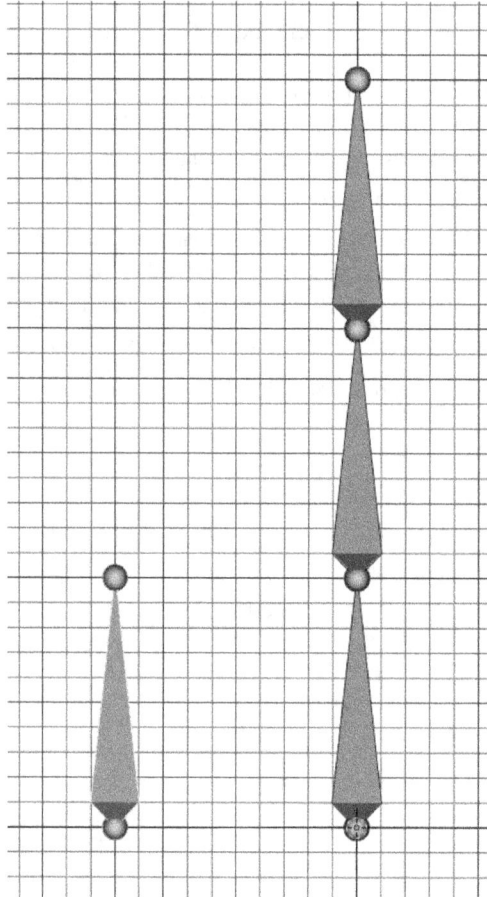

Figure 2.8 – Starting the next bone chain

Quick tip

Hold *Ctrl* and see how it changes your inputs when moving, rotating, and scaling. The bone should snap to the grid and transform in increments. So, if you're wondering how I keep my elements perfectly aligned, this is how. I enabled the grid in *Figure 2.8* so you can see this.

4. Extend the left bone into a chain just as we did before by extruding the tail along the *Z* axis to end up with something like this:

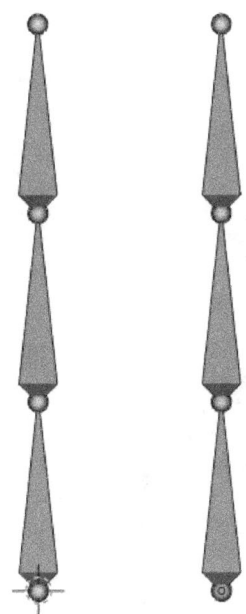

Figure 2.9 – Two bone chains

> **Quick shortcuts**
> *E*: **Extrude**, *G*: **Grab**, *R*: **Rotate**, *Ctrl*: **Snapping**

In this section, we added an armature, entered edit mode, extruded, and added more bones. Now we are going to finish this chapter with **Pose Mode**. Bones aren't much use if we can't pose them as per our requirements.

Using Pose Mode

These bones aren't of much use if we can't bend them to our will. Enter pose mode. As the name might suggest, this mode allows us to pose bones. We need to enter Pose mode, select a bone, and rotate it. You should already have a rough idea of how to do this, but here are step-by-step instructions:

1. Press *Tab* or use the dropdown to enter **Pose** mode.

2. Left-click on any bone and take note of the outline.

3. Press *R* to rotate the selected bone, using your mouse to rotate:

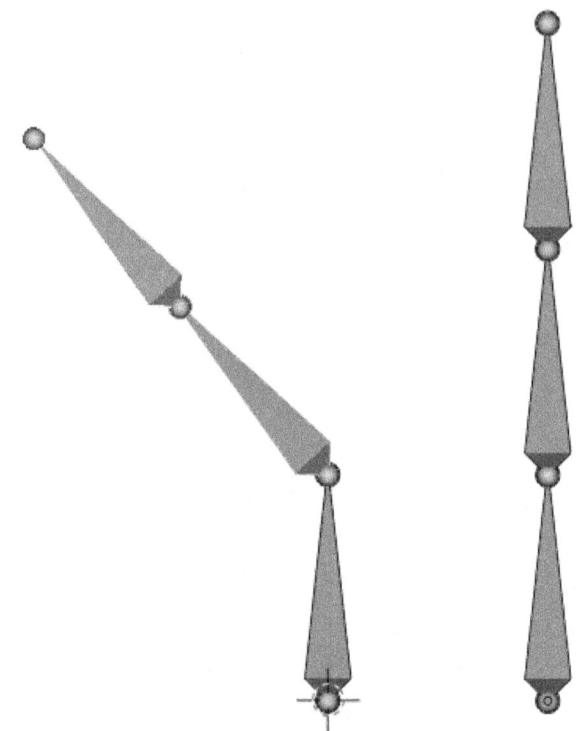

Figure 2.10 – Rotating bone (FK)

Take note of how rotating a bone will affect the bones above it but not below it. Bending the bones one by one is known as **Forward Kinematics** (**FK**). We will be able to compare it to IK later.

Just like how we can limit transforms to an axis by pressing G to grab and pressing Z to limit to the Z axis, we can do this in pose mode too!

More on transforms

Using a single press of an axis while transforming an object will use the global coordinates. Essentially, this is the orientation or the scene. Z will always point up, while X and Y will always point in their own directions.

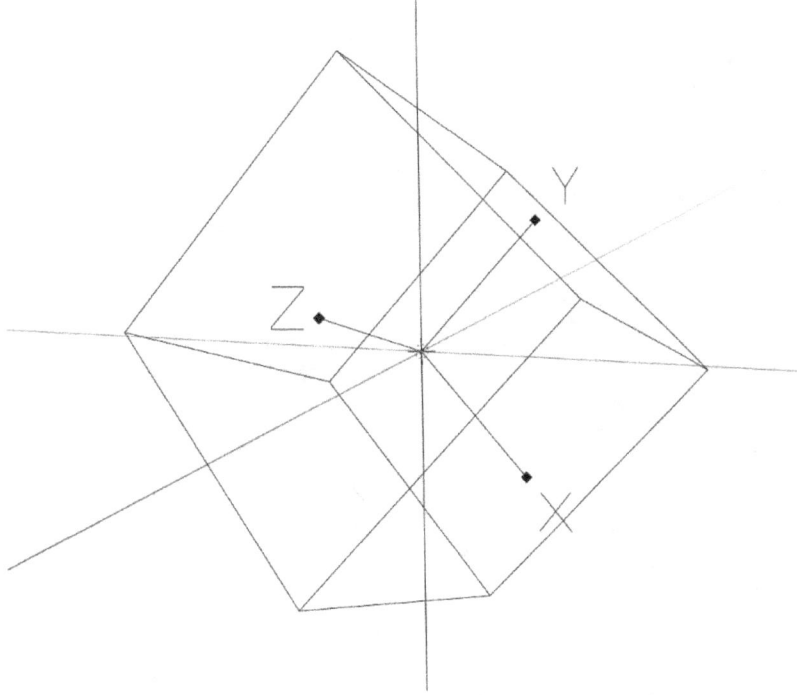

Figure 2.11 – Local transforms

This image shows the **LOCAL** axis. Every object has its own coordinate system. This is attached to the object. If you rotate any object, its local coordinates will follow. It's like the object's own little world that it takes with it wherever it goes.

You can access these coordinates when transforming an object by double-tapping the required axis. Take the following example.

Pressing *G* + *Z* twice will enter the local coordinates. Do this yourself with a rotated object and Blender will highlight the coordinates being used.

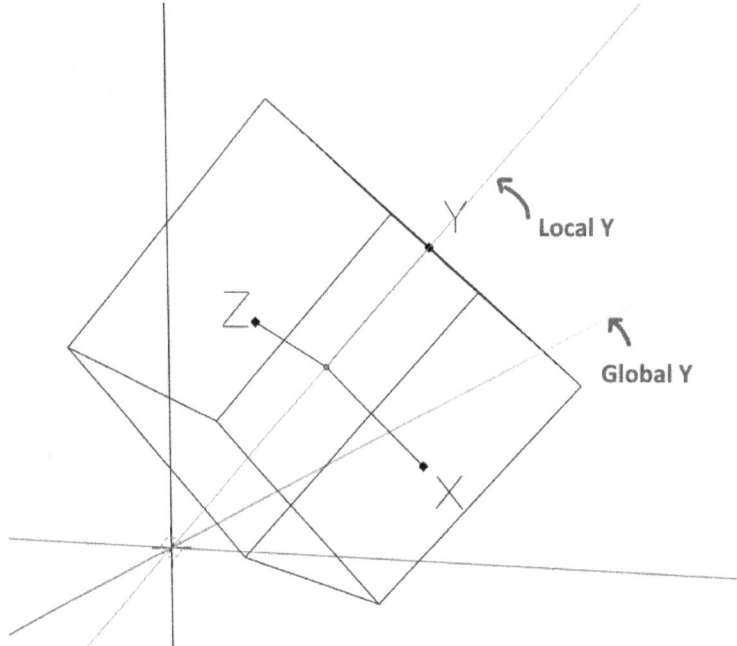

Figure 2.12 – Local axis following object

Any transform done in object mode can be reset using *Alt*:

- *Alt* + *G* will reset the location
- *Alt* + *R* will reset the rotation
- *Alt* + *S* will reset the scale

Everything mentioned about **GLOBAL** and **LOCAL** and clearing transforms applies to bones in pose mode too. Any transforms done in pose mode will not carry over into edit mode. This is really useful when putting a rigged model into a stress position and switching between pose Mode and edit mode to track changes. This will become apparent as you become familiar with the process.

You might think most of this is for animators, but when rigging, you will also need to pose your work. By posing your work, you can test for defects or insufficient results before it reaches the rest of the team. That's important for keeping the work smooth and reducing the pass (revision) count you will need to make on your work.

Summary

That's a wrap for this chapter! We started this chapter by learning how to add objects by placing your mouse in the 3D viewport, pressing *Shift + A* to bring up the Add object menu, and choosing **Armature**. After that, we learned how to select objects in our viewport by using mouse controls and how to deselect objects (or select all) with a shortcut key. Then, we moved on to learn how our view can be changed and about the different view parameters, such as panning, zooming, and focusing on objects to orbit them. After learning about how to change our view, we saw how we can place bones in our viewport by entering **Edit** mode, either with the dropdown or using *Tab*, to add bones to an armature object. Finally, we ended the chapter by looking at pose mode and how it can be used to adjust bones, using the same transform controls as normal object mode, *G R*, and *S*.

The next chapter will cover weight painting, telling parts of the mesh to follow specified bones, all with the stroke of a paintbrush (sort of). There's a little more on the viewport controls and a little theory on how weight painting works.

Because of the large number of shortcuts covered in this chapter, I have summarized them in the following table for you as a quick reference, should you need them:

Alt + R	Reset transform
E	Extrude
G	Grab
R	Rotate
Ctrl	Snapping/Incremental
. (Number pad)	Focus
Scroll wheel	Zoom
MMB (scroll wheel clicked in)	Pan
MMB + Shift	Lateral
Alt + MMB	Orthographic views

Table 2.1 - Shortcuts

Part 2: Rigging

Part 2 features the bulk of the book, focusing on both the placement of bones and weight painting. It also covers all the rigging basics.

This part has the following chapters:

- *Chapter 3, Using Weighting Tools to Give Life to a Mesh*
- *Chapter 4, Beginning the Rigging Process*
- *Chapter 5, Getting Started with Weight Painting*

3

Using Weighting Tools to Give Life to a Mesh

In the previous chapter, we added objects, selected them, and edited them in **Edit Mode** while moving our view around in the 3D viewport.

In this chapter, we will start by adding a mesh to the scene. We will enter **Edit Mode**, make loop cuts, extrude and scale, and cover basic transforms in **Edit Mode**. We will learn more about our view and the modes we can use to get more information and a clearer view of our work. Then, we will use the correct parent constraint to set us up for the most important topic in this book, weight painting.

In this chapter, we will cover the following:

- Creating a mesh
- Prelude to painting

By the end of this chapter, you will be prepared for weight painting correctly and be able to use its basic tools to assign weights to vertices with the correct bones selected.

Creating a mesh

We can't do any weight painting without a mesh; that much should be clear to anyone. There are, however, some important steps to take that will prevent headaches in the future, such as placing vertices in optimal places to support quality deformation. If the mesh is constructed poorly, no matter how perfect your weight painting, it will be impossible to get a good result.

To start, we need to add some mesh to our scene. We will go over some terminology once we have done this. Follow these steps:

1. To start, make sure you are in **Object Mode** (*Tab*, or dropdown), go ahead and bring up the **Add object** menu with *Shift + A*, then navigate to **Mesh | Cube** and add a cube. Your scene should look as follows:

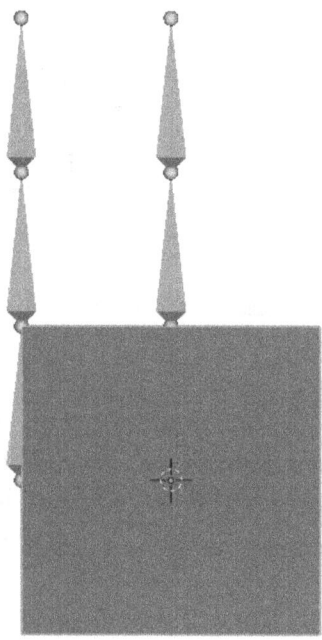

Figure 3.1 – Cube added to our scene

2. We want this cube to be a tower in between our bones. To do this, we're going to go into **Edit Mode** and make sure we have selected **Vertice** mode. The blue icon next to the mode dropdown depicts **Vertice** mode:

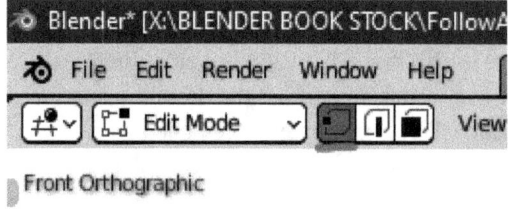

Figure 3.2 – Vertice mode selected

Before moving on, here is some very important information regarding how armature deformation works, so read it carefully.

The basic concept of armature deformation is that by assigning **weights** to the vertices, we can tell vertices which bones to follow and by how much. This is how our mesh will follow the bones smoothly. Without this ability, everything would be a rigid collection of shapes with clear joins and separations – not very organic or visually appealing.

When weighing, each bone will have a **Weight** group; this group contains all the vertices and how much authority a parent bone has over each vertex. Only vertices can be in these lists. In reality, only vertices deform in a mesh; the edges and faces just follow along. So, when we want deformation, we *need* vertices. Follow along and you will see this firsthand.

3.   In **Edit Mode**, with the whole cube highlighted in orange by pressing *A* (a single *A* press selects all and a double press deselects all), grab the mesh and place it roughly in between our bones. Press *S* to scale it down to an acceptable level, like so:

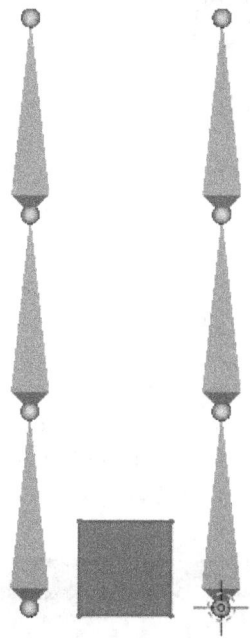

Figure 3.3 – Mesh placed between two chains of bones

Next, we want our cube to be as tall as the bones, as shown in *Figure 3.6*. To do this, we could select the top face and extrude, but a better way of doing this would be to grab the top face and instead drag it up.

So, now that we have a scene set up with everything, we need to start weight painting. We're not quite ready to start weight painting though, as you will notice that we currently only have a mesh for the lowest bones; we need more mesh to deform for the rest of the bones.

In the next section, before we complete the mesh, we're going to cover views in more depth. You can't make what you can't see, so it's important we get the best view we can.

When changing views in our current viewport display mode, we can only select the vertices in front of us, not the ones hidden behind.

Blender has four main display modes: **Wireframe**, **Solid**, **Material**, and **Render**. Their names are self-explanatory for the most part.

Wireframe will display edges and nothing more, which is great for seeing through our objects straight to the bones. **Solid** displays all faces in solid color, which is good for observing how the mesh is deforming. We don't need to use the last two, **Material** and **Render**, so you can forget them for now.

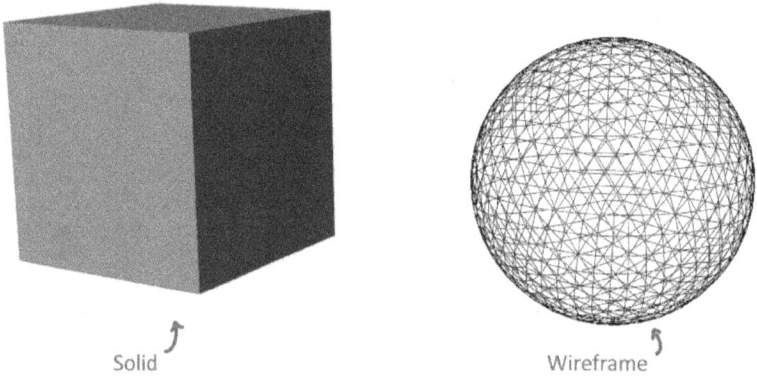

Solid   Wireframe

Figure 3.4 – Viewport display modes

In our case, we need **Wireframe** and **Transparency** so that we may see through the cube. Remember this as it will be very important for many aspects of our work. In *Figure 3.5*, you can see the four display modes represented as spheres in the top right of the UI; select the **Wireframe** sphere and the **Transparency** button on the left of it as well (it depicts two squares overlapping), and notice the viewport changing.

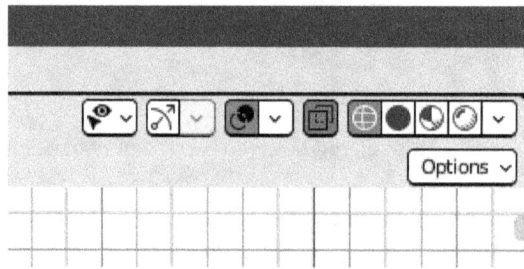

Figure 3.5 – Viewport display modes

Note that we don't strictly need **Wireframe**, but using **Wireframe** removes a lot of useless visual information; it's the transparency that ultimately lets us see and select through objects. If you're not sure why we use **Transparency** along with **Wireframe**, you can go ahead and try selecting other view modes; you will soon realize that **Wireframe** is our best bet for seeing and selecting through a mesh.

We need to select the top four vertices on the top of the cube. We're in front view at the moment so we can only see two, but thanks to **Wireframe** and **Transparency**, we can just select these top two and the ones behind it will be selected, but *only if we use area select*. A normal mouse click can only ever select one item at a time. With our viewport set up for selecting through a mesh, we have greatly reduced the number of button presses and clicks needed to select vertices. Selecting the front will also select the back; this is explained next as we go over selection modes.

Selection modes

Blender has many different selection modes; the ones to note are **Brush select**, **Box select**, and **Lasso**. **Box select** and **Lasso** should be self-explanatory to anyone who is familiar with other PC editor programs. **Brush select** can be better described as area select; this will show a circle area around your mouse and let you paint over items and select them all.

To use **Box select**, simply press *B*, and you will notice dotted lines appear. These draw from your mouse to the edge of the viewport and are there to help you align your selection with the elements. It's as simple as clicking and dragging to select what you want (make sure everything is deselected first).

Brush select is far more versatile, so it's a good idea to get used to it. It allows us to select a group of vertices by painting over them with an adjustable brush at great speed and precision. Press *C* to bring the brush up; you can use the scroll wheel to adjust its size. Click and drag to paint over vertices and select them; once done, press *Esc* to end the selection.

The final selection mode is **Lasso**. Hold *Ctrl + RMB* to start drawing; simply surround what you want to select, then let go of *RMB* to select.

To recap: We have added a mesh and relocated it to a suitable position in **Edit Mode**. We have also been introduced to more viewport controls that will enable us to work at greater speeds, notably the **Transparency** and **Wireframe** view modes. Continue by editing this new mesh with loop cuts to make geometry that will allow us to deform it.

Quick shortcuts
B: **Box select**, *C*: **Brush select**, *Ctrl + RMB*: **Lasso select**, *Esc*: leave selection mode

Continuing with vertices

With selection out of the way, let's get back to the task at hand, namely, getting this cube to the same height as the bones, and creating more geometry for the bones to deform.

Select the top vertices, press G | Z, and push the mouse up to get the cube to the same height as the bones, like so:

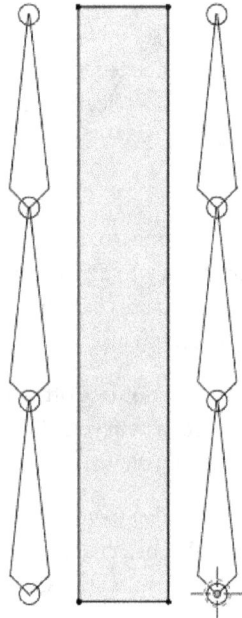

Figure 3.6 – Top vertices placed at the same height as the bones

You can hold *MMB* and pan your view at any time to get a better view of your work. Just make sure to return to **Front View** for these instructions.

As mentioned before, we need vertices to deform this mesh. As it stands, there are no vertices in the middle of this; therefore, the bones at the sides have nothing to deform. Follow along and we will fix this with loop cuts.

Adding loops

A loop cut is a ring of vertices we can add to any mesh made of quads (faces made of four vertices). It's essentially a way of adding more geometry in a clean way.

While in **Edit Mode**, press *Ctrl + R*; we are now in loop cut mode. Hover your mouse in the middle of the mesh and notice a yellow line appear like so:

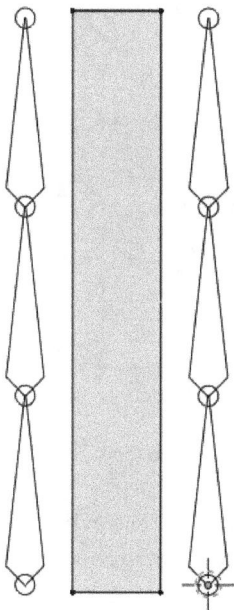

Figure 3.7 – Yellow line showing cut placement

Ideally, we want a loop of vertices per joint for this example (as in *Figure 3.7*). With the loop cut tool, we can use the scroll wheel to adjust the number of cuts. If you roll the scroll wheel up one notch, you should see two cuts appear, roughly in line with the joints of the bones.

Go ahead and confirm this cut with *LMB*; you should see this cut change color. When it changes color, this means you have applied it but are still holding onto it. You will also notice that your cursor changes to a set of arrows. We don't want to move this cut; let's keep it symmetrical and try not to mess it up. Press *Esc* or *RMB* to let go of the loops. By adding loops, we can make more geometry to allow our mesh to deform.

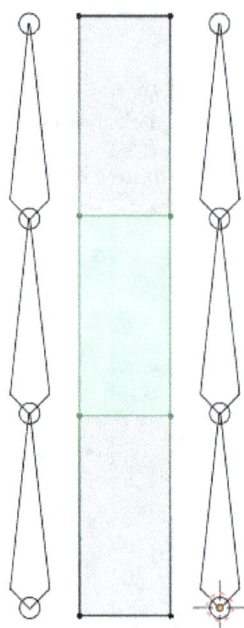

Figure 3.8 – Two loop cuts placed

If you do this correctly, you will notice dots at the end of the lines. These are the new vertices we have made, which are roughly in line with the joints of the bones.

> **Quick shortcuts**
>
> *Ctrl + R*: Loop cut

Now we have an armature, consisting of two chains of bones, and a mesh with geometry in the correct places to support deformation. We just need to tie these two together by using an **Armature Deform** parent type.

Prelude to painting

Now let's get into the bulk of our work, weight painting.

Firstly, we need to parent the mesh to the armature, so that Blender knows that the mesh belongs to the bones. If we didn't do this, we couldn't assign our weights to the bones.

Here's how we parent our object to the armature:

1. Ensure you are in **Object Mode**.

2. Select the **Mesh** *first* (order is important).

3. Select the bones with *Shift + RMB*.

4. Press *Ctrl + P*.

    In *Figure 3.9*, we can see the **Set Parent To** menu:

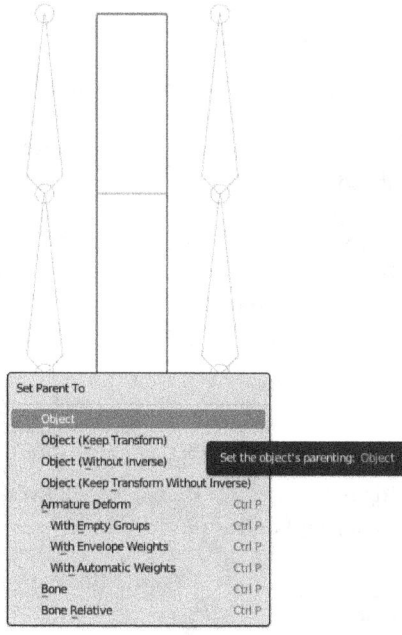

Figure 3.9 – Set Parent To menu

There are multiple entries here in the menu, all of which do something different. The first set of options are related to simple object parent relations and are of no concern to us right now, but in case you are wondering, here's a brief description of each:

*   **Object**: The child objects will inherit the transformations of the parent.

*   **Object (Keep Transform)**: The child objects will remember any previous transformations applied to them from the previous parent object.

*   **Object (Without Inverse)**: Assign a parent without moving the child object.

*   **Object (Keep Transform Without Inverse)**: The object will move to the location of the parent but keep its rotation and scale.

After the **Object** entries, we get to the **Armature** options; these are important for our operation:

- **Armature Deform**: Simply uses the armature to deform an object (with empty weights).

- **With Empty Groups**: Does not generate any vertex groups. None of the vertices is registered by the bones; you have a clean slate.

- **With Envelope Weights**: Automatically define weights based on an envelope area around the bones.

- **With Automatic Weights**: Automatically define weights based on the distance to the bone.

- **Bone**: Same as **Object** but for bones and mesh.

- **Bone Relative**: Same as **Bone** but with the current delta taken into account.

While this may be a lot of information to take in, the reality is that we will only be using one of these options, **Armature Deform**. Go ahead and select this option.

With Automatic Weights is a tricky one to use. Sometimes it works flawlessly, but more often than not, you will be spending more time fixing the mess it creates than if you just started with **Armature Deform**. This book will not cover With **Automatic Weights**. Once you understand the basics of weight painting, you may find yourself able to use With **Automatic Weights**, but right now it's more hassle than it's worth.

With Envelope Weights is for use in very niche circumstances. With **Envelope Weights** gives you the ability to mark bones as *deform bones* and set their radius of control. It's incredibly quick to use but also wildly impractical for anything more complex than a worm. Every tool in Blender has its uses but we don't need any tool other than **Empty Groups** for now.

After selecting this, you won't see much happen. So, to verify this has worked, grab the armature and drag it around; the mesh should follow.

Armature deform modifier

Ctrl + P is one of Blender's many shortcuts, but what exactly does it do? In short, it adds an armature deform modifier to the mesh and sets the target of this modifier as the bones.

The following figure shows the modifier we just added. You don't need to touch it for now but it's good to know where it is (and that it exists):

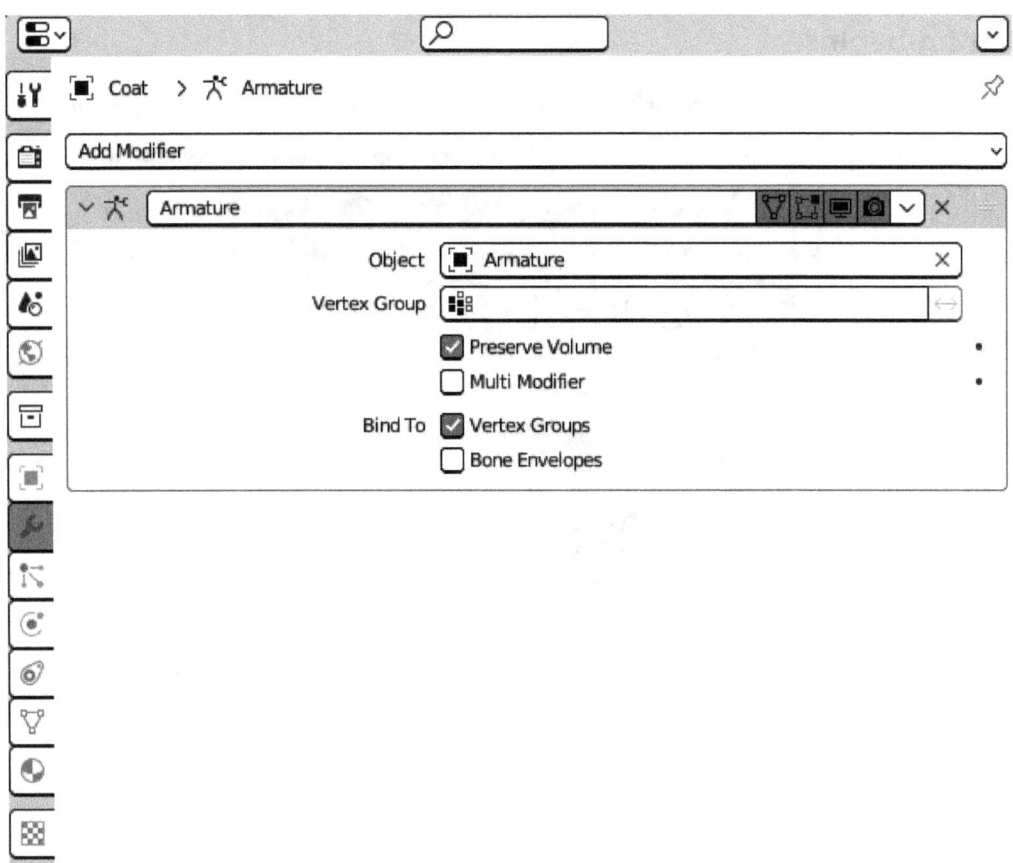

Figure 3.10 – Deform modifier

> **Quick shortcuts**
>
> *Ctrl + P*: **Parent** menu

With our mesh parented to the armature, using **Empty Groups**, we can get started on weight painting the bulk of the work.

Painting begins

If you remember how important our selection order was, entering **Weight Paint** mode is the same.

Select **Armature** first and M**esh** second, and use the top-left dropdown to select **Weight Paint**:

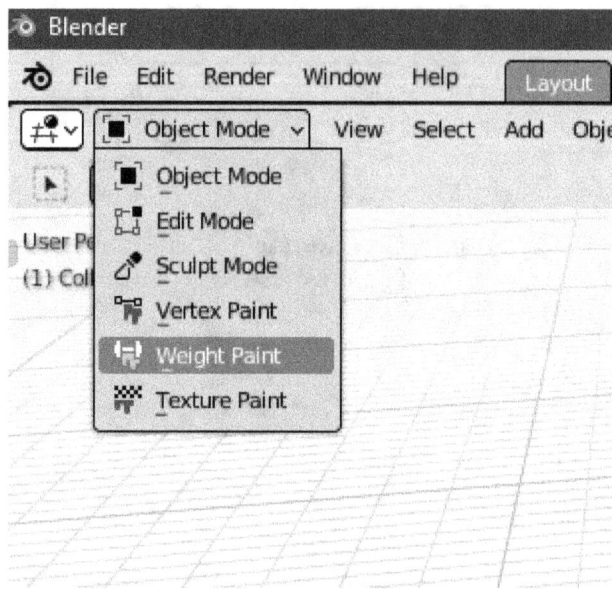

Figure 3.11 – Weight Paint mode

After entering **Weight Paint** mode, you will notice several things in the UI change:

- **Mesh**: The mesh is now blue, as shown in *Figure 3.9*, or *cold*. This represents a weight value of 0; we will cover these terms in more detail later.

- **UI**: New UI elements for painting modes and settings have appeared down the left side and across the top; I will point these out in greater detail shortly.

- **Cursor**: The cursor has changed to a circle. This is our brush, which we will use to paint our weights.

The top toolbar of your UI will change to what is pictured in *Figure 3.12*; these new controls are as follows:

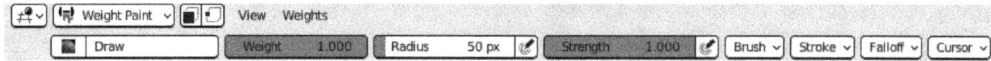

Figure 3.12 – Weight Paint brush options

- **Brush paint mode**: Choose how the brush behaves, from adding to already existing values to multiplying, mixing, dividing, and more. For the purpose of simplicity, we will stick to **Draw**. You can read more here if you so desire: `https://docs.blender.org/manual/en/latest/sculpt_paint/weight_paint/tools.html`.

- **Weight** and **Strength**: These values assign painted vertices between 0 and 1. If we assume a strength of 1 and we are painting onto a cold (or zero) vertex, then the weight applied will be what we set. The **Weight** value defines the target weight that will eventually be reached when you paint long enough on the same location of the mesh. The strength value determines how many strokes you need to place at the target weight.

- **Radius**: This option changes how big our brush is. You can view the size in real time by observing your cursor size, as it is a circle that represents our brush size. Radius is useful for getting fine control or blanketing a whole area with a larger radius.

In *Figure 3.13*, you can see a stroke option. The following screenshot shows this option expanded out:

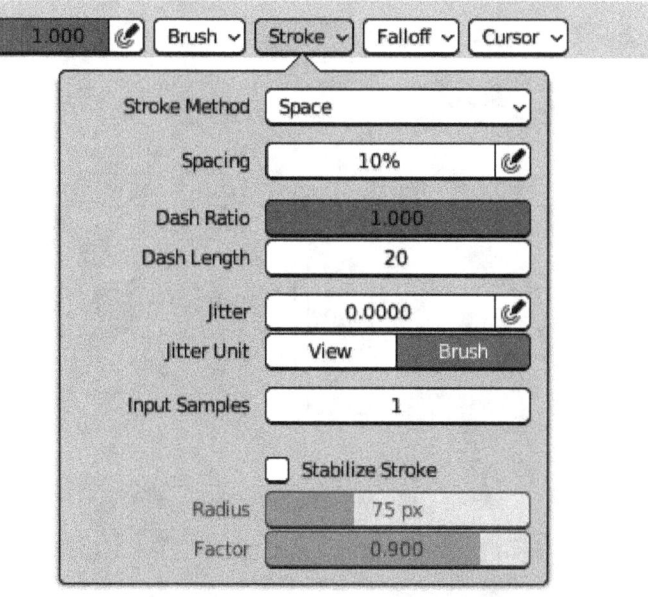

Figure 3.13 – Stroke brush options

This dropdown has a host of helpful control options. However, we will not be covering them as we do not need them. These controls are more orientated toward texture painting and sculpting.

The same can be said for **Falloff**. It is not very useful to us as at this time; it gives options to control the amount of brush applied from the middle to the outside.

Cursor has the option to turn the cursor off or to change the color.

If you're ever curious, you can try playing with them or reading the Blender documentation, `https://docs.blender.org/manual/en/latest`, where every button is explained.

In *Figure 3.13*, there are more tools for sculpting, texture painting, and weight painting. The two primary tools you will use are **Paint** (selected and blue) and **Blur** (below the **Paint** option). The rest can be ignored:

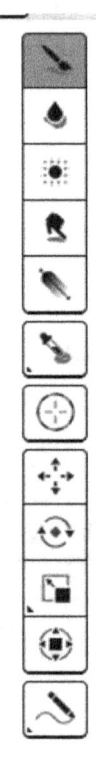

Figure 3.14 – More brush options

Painting

Coming up are step-by-step instructions. It's vital you understand what we're about to cover, so take it slow if needed:

1. We're going to assign our first weights. Go ahead and select the bottom-left bone in **Pose Mode**. This is as easy as left-clicking, but because we are in **Weight Paint** mode, we must use *Shift + LMB*. This is due to the fact that a simple left-click is used for painting in this mode.

2. Then click on the bottom-left corner to paint our first weights.

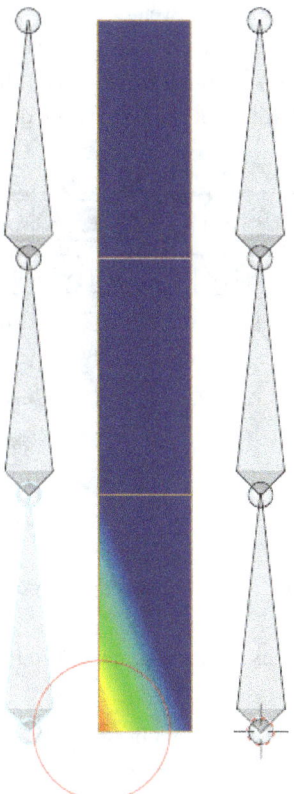

Figure 3.15 – Weight-painted vertex

Note that we select the bone, then paint. We do not want to paint on the wrong bone weight group. We need to select the bone we want to paint on. It's easy to forget this and waste time painting onto the wrong bone.

The way the weights are shown is pretty logical:

- **Red/hot**: Full weight or `1.0`

- **Blue/cold**: No weight or `0.0`

A value of `1` means that the bone will have complete authority over the vertex; it will pull it with a 1:1 force. Wherever the bone goes, the vertex goes.

A value of `0` means the bone has no control over the vertex.

Anything between hot and cold is used to visualize values between `1` and `0`. In the preceding figure, the yellow/green would show `0.5`; however, there are no verts there, so it doesn't apply to anything.

3. In *Figure 3.16*, you can see more options for weight painting; in the dropdown is **Auto Normalize**. In short, this prevents a single vertex from having more than 1.0 weight. Say we select two separate bones and paint 1.0 onto the same vertex; it will shift the weight to make sure that the weights do not exceed 1.0. We will look at this in more detail later. Go ahead and enable this:

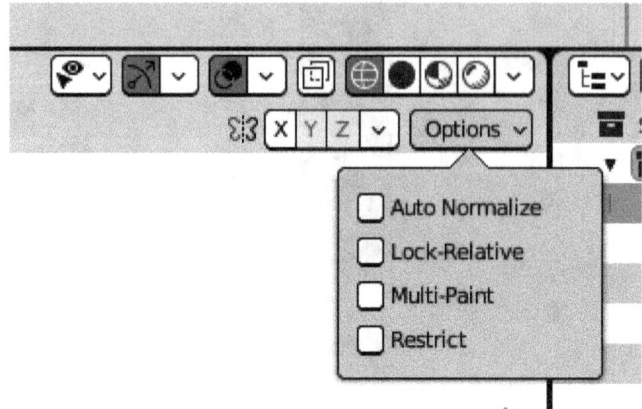

Figure 3.16 – More painting options

4. Go ahead and paint the next vertex up, the one closest to the tip of the selected bone (keeping the first bone selected).

5. Staying on the left bone chain, select the next bone up. We're going to paint the vert next to the tip of this bone too. You might wonder why we don't paint the base too, but that will become clear when you start to pose the bones.

6. Select the top bone on the left chain and paint the top-left vertex.

7. If you make a mistake and wish to erase (set weights back to cold), you can set the weight option of the brush, pictured in *Figure 3.12*, to 0 – this acts as your eraser.

8. Start selecting the right chain of bones and do the same, effectively mirroring both sides.

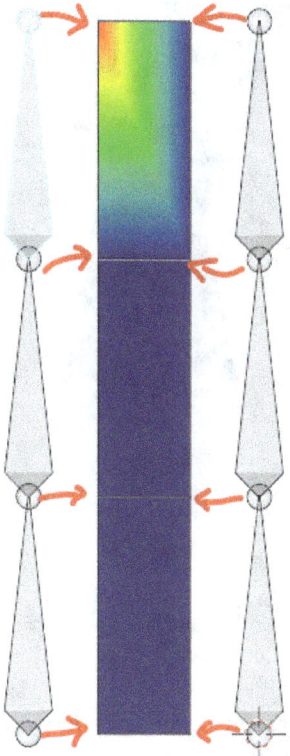

Figure 3.17 – Diagram to show what to paint

Use the preceding figure as a guide. Don't be afraid to make mistakes or to figure out things for yourself; that's all part of learning.

With weights added, let's check to see whether it worked. It's a good idea to get comfortable with the process of checking your weights as you work.

Posing in Weight Paint mode

After you have painted all the vertices, you can go ahead and start rotating the bones and watch how they distort the mesh. Remember: select a bone, press *R*, and move the mouse to rotate. In *Figure 3.18*, you can see weights in action. The vertices follow their respective bones and any cold vertices do not move; the vertices at the back of the cube do not move at all, as we have not weight-painted them:

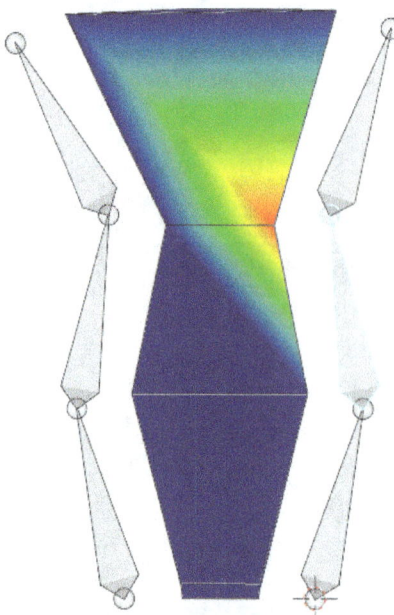

Figure 3.18 – Bones posed randomly

Select all bones (*A*), and reset their transform with *Alt + R*. We are going to give two bones control over one vertex and watch the fight commence. Note we enabled **Auto Normalize**, so even if we paint 1.0 twice onto the same vertex, the result will be 0.5, showing as green. This makes the weights simple, intuitive, and easy to understand; otherwise, when we select a single bone, it might show red on the areas where two bones have 1.0 weight.

We will carry out a short exercise in the next section.

Exercise

This exercise will show how a vertex can be shared between more than one bone.

Select the top-left bone (*Shift + LMB*) and paint the top-right vertex. This top-right vertex is now under left-bone and right-bone control with 1.0 for both. Rotate either of these bones and watch how the vertex averages between the bones. The math isn't important in the slightest but here's a small rundown:

- One vertex under the control of two bones, each with 1.0, will produce a weight of 0.5 between each, resulting in the vertex being in the middle, because no bone has more control over the other

- A split of 0.75 to 0.25 between two bones will result in the vertex sitting ¾ toward the 0.75 bone

- A split of 0.1 to 0.1 will still produce a half split because, again, no bone has more control

Note that this math is calculated and applied when **Auto Normalize** is enabled, so if we paint 1.0 for two separate bones, Blender will correct us and set the weights to 0.5. Without **Auto Normalize**, the weights would remain at 1.0 and we would have a much harder time.

Remember too that a vertex can be controlled by more than just two bones; the same idea applies, as previously mentioned.

Again, do not worry if you don't get the math. It's really not important; I have included it to explain the mechanics behind the art.

Take a look at *Figure 3.19*. It's the knee of a character that has been weight-painted to give a soft transition between the upper and lower half of the leg. Making a transition is quite simple, but very important.

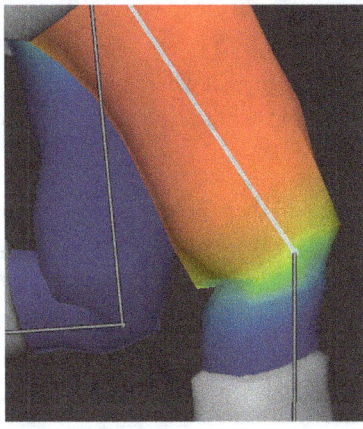

Figure 3.19 – Thigh bone with weight falloff

Figure 3.20 shows a gradient between two bones. This is exactly how the knee is set up in *Figure 3.19*; this smooth handoff between bones is what a large part of weight painting is about. We're going to give this handoff between bones a shot in our final workpiece for this chapter.

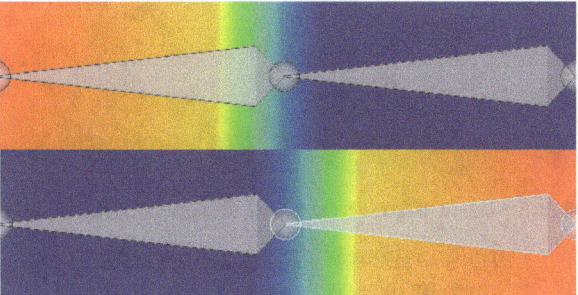

Figure 3.20 – Example of gradients between bones

To recap: After learning how to select bones and assign weights, we're next going to observe how a single vertex can be weighted to multiple bones. In effect, one vertex being averaged between multiple bones can give a smooth granular result.

Final piece

In this exercise, we will take our previous mesh and give it a central spine, weight painting the whole of the volume to a bone chain.

Follow these steps:

1.   Enter **Object Mode** and delete the armature (the bones).

2.   Press *Shift + A* and add an armature.

3.   As the previous mesh had bones assigned, it will remember them and think our new bones are the old ones and will keep their old weights. To get rid of them, follow these steps, depicted in *Figure 3.21*:

      I.   Select **Object** data properties, then **Vertex groups**, then press the – button to remove each vertex. This comes in handy when a bone is behaving in a strange manner, and you would rather scrap all the weights on the bone and start again. Selecting the relevant bone and painting will create a vertex group if one does not already exist/has been deleted.

      II.   There's also a + button for adding vertex groups but this is of no use to us; its use lies outside rigging. Again, painting when there is no vertex group will automatically create one.

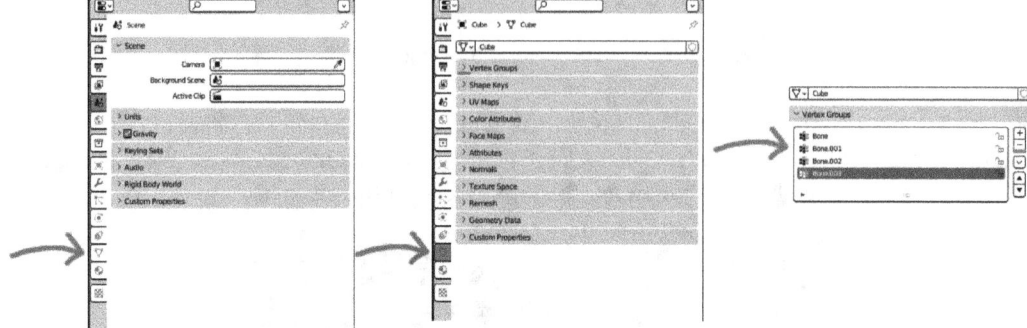

Figure 3.21 – Storyboard of steps taken to delete weights

4.   Use *G* to grab, and move the armature to the bottom center of the mesh.

5.   Enter **Edit Mode** and extrude this bone into a chain, making a new bone at every vertex loop. Remember to press *E* followed by the axis you want to extrude along, and using *Ctrl* will snap to the grid.

6.   Enter **Object Mode**, then select the mesh and then the bone and parent with empty groups (With **Automatic Weights** works wonders here, but we are going to paint it by hand anyway).

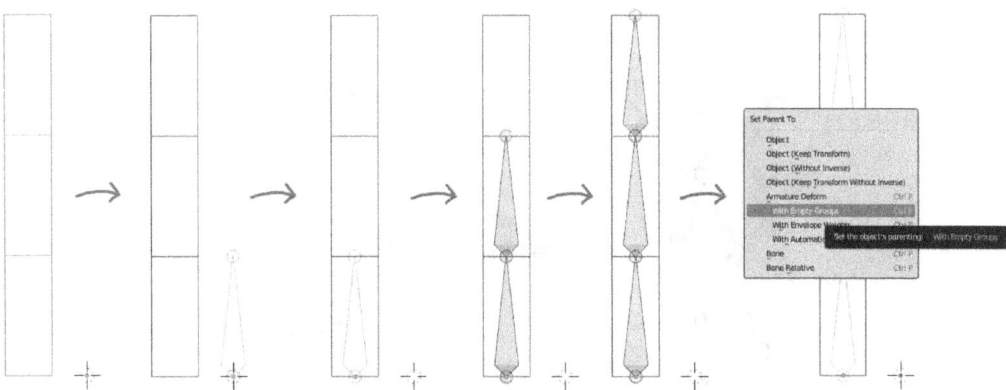

Figure 3.22 – Storyboard of steps taken

7. Select the bone, then select the mesh and enter **Weight Paint** mode; we are ready to paint.

8. Start from the bottom with a brush weight of 1.0, and paint all four vertices on the bottom. We discussed how to move your view around earlier on; you will need to do so to get a better view of the bottom of the mesh, and the rest as we continue to paint upward.

9. Move up to the next joint and set the brush strength to 0.5. Keeping the first bone selected, paint this loop. The first and second bone are going to share this loop, so we will give them both a strength of 0.5. If you cast your mind back to the math earlier, 1.0 and 1.0 would have the same effect; cast your mind further back and you will remember we enabled **Auto Normalize**. So, in theory, we could paint with 1.0 and Blender would set it to 0.5 for us. But it's best we don't for good practice.

10. Now for the next bone. It has to share with both the bottom and top, so let's give all the vertices around its joints a weight of 0.5.

11. Finish with the top bone, having 0.5 on its lower joint and 1.0 at the top.

Remember we're working in 3D for this part; get that camera spinning!

It should look something like this:

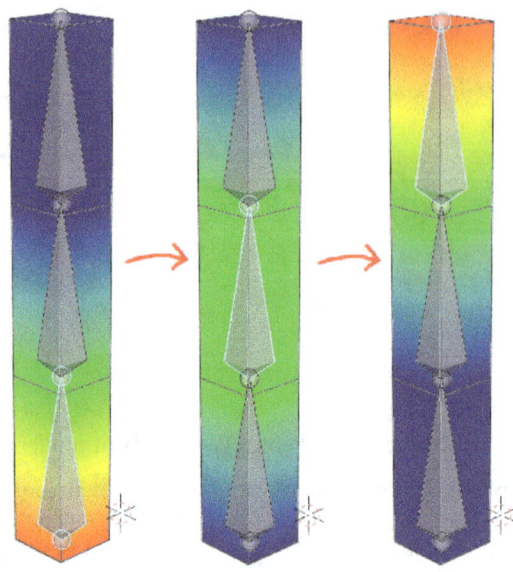

Figure 3.23 – Steps taken to weight paint the cuboid

The following figure specifies the details of our results:

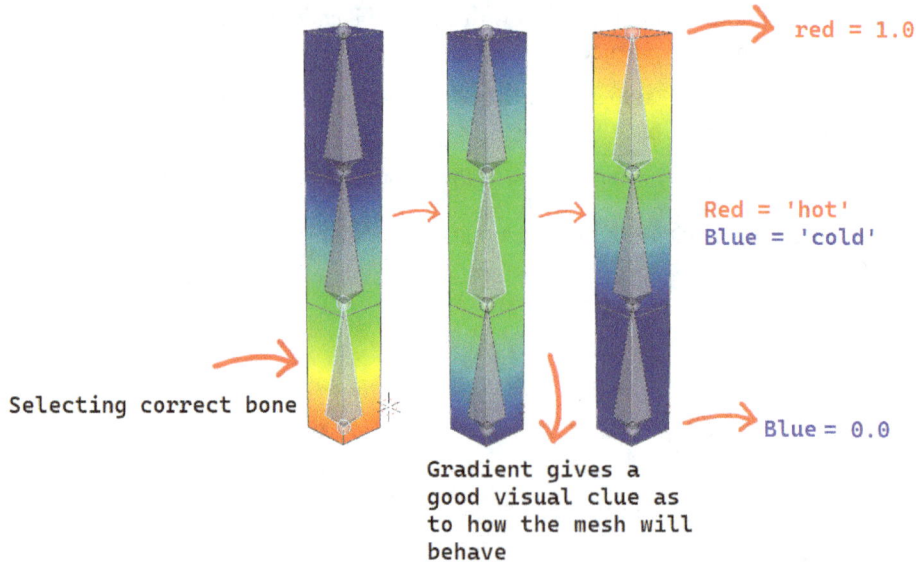

Figure 3.24 – Visual recap

Go ahead and select any bone and press *R* to rotate it. You can play around with your result; it's not perfect (lack of geometry is to blame here), but it has come out as a success!

Summary

We started the chapter by learning about the basic terminology for Blender, that is, bones, meshes, and weights:

- The head is the joint placed at the wider part of the bone; the tail is the thinner part

- Weights range from 0 to 1.0, or from *cold* to *hot*

- We can bring up the **Add Object** menu with *Shift + A*

- We can scale (*S*), rotate (*R*), and transform (*G*) any selected item

We added both a cube and an armature to the scene with the **Add objects** pop-up menu and entered **Edit Mode** (*Tab*), or we could have used the dropdown pictured in *Figure 2.3* in *Chapter 2*.

Once in **Edit Mode**, for both the mesh and armature, we cut, scaled, transformed, and extruded (*E*) to form two towers of bones with mesh in between.

We then learned how to get set up for weight painting by pressing *Ctrl + P* after selecting the mesh *before* the bone. Finally, we weight-painted a mesh by selecting the correct bones and used the ability to pose bones in **Weight Paint** mode to verify that our painting had worked.

In the next chapter, we're going to start rigging a human model, from placing bones and creating a skeleton to adding weights and exploring shape keys and drivers.

4

Beginning the Rigging Process

In *Chapter 3*, we added and prepared a mesh for rigging, and we covered the core fundamentals of rigging. In this chapter, we are going to start rigging a human model. We will start by making sure to set up both the mesh and the armature correctly to avoid problems that can be hard to fix, or even diagnose, later down the line. Then, we will be placing the needed bones in the correct places to fashion ourselves a skeletal control that we can tie our human mesh to.

In this chapter, we will cover the following topics:

- Understanding the core ideas behind rigging

- Setting up the model

- Starting the rigging process

- Naming and mirroring

By the end of this chapter, you will be able to fully rig a human model. You'll have learned how to place an armature, how to add bones to it, and how to name them correctly to avoid any confusion while rigging models.

Understanding the core ideas behind rigging

Before we start with this chapter, we should learn about the two core ideas of rigging:

- **Study your subject!** It's important to understand how your subject moves in the first place. While this might be obvious for a human character, there's a good chance you will encounter otherworldly masses of mesh that will require coordination with multiple team members or a little bit of creativity. Failure to give thought to this may lead to wasted hours as you may backtrack on mistakes you could have ironed out before starting.

- **Stress and iterate!** Once you think you are done, pose the whole rig into stressful poses. Placing bones into typical use case poses (being careful to not move them outside their intended range of motion) will reveal weak spots and deficiencies in any work. Bones might pull the wrong parts of the mesh or deformations may not match expectations when the rig is moved. A static pose provides no information on the quality of your work, rendering you completely blind.

We need a human to rig. You could use your own material or the sample I have provided here: `https://github.com/PacktPublishing/3D-Character-Rigging-in-Blender`.

If you installed Blender correctly, `.blend` files should open upon a double-click. This should give you the model shown in the following figure:

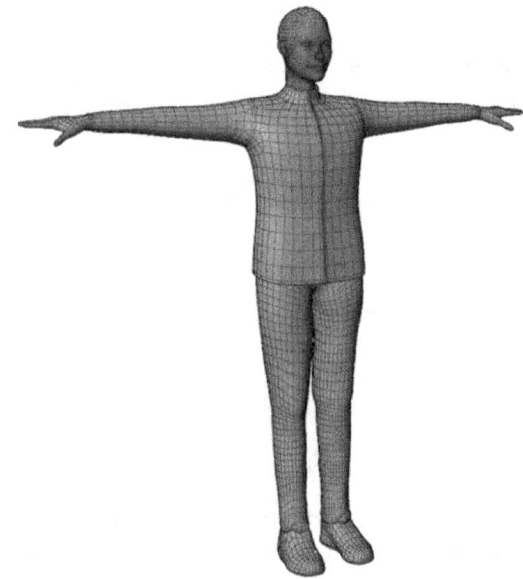

Figure 4.1 – Provided human model

It's recommended that you use this model for now as it will make it easier to follow along. + If you have a model that you want to rig then you can by all means use it. Theres very little that is model specific, just as long as it's a basic human you should have no trouble following this book.

Setting up the model

Before we go on to rigging and weighting, you need to be aware of some common pitfalls that can occur even before starting work. So, I will show you how to prepare the mesh you will be working with. Just before we continue placing our bones, we need to prep the model. Different people produce models differently and it's up to us to deal with this. Issues such as scale, rotation, and object origins can cause massive headaches if we don't deal with them before we begin.

Fixing scale, rotation, and origin

Select all the objects we are going to rig, press *Ctrl + A* with your mouse inside the viewport, and select **All Transforms**:

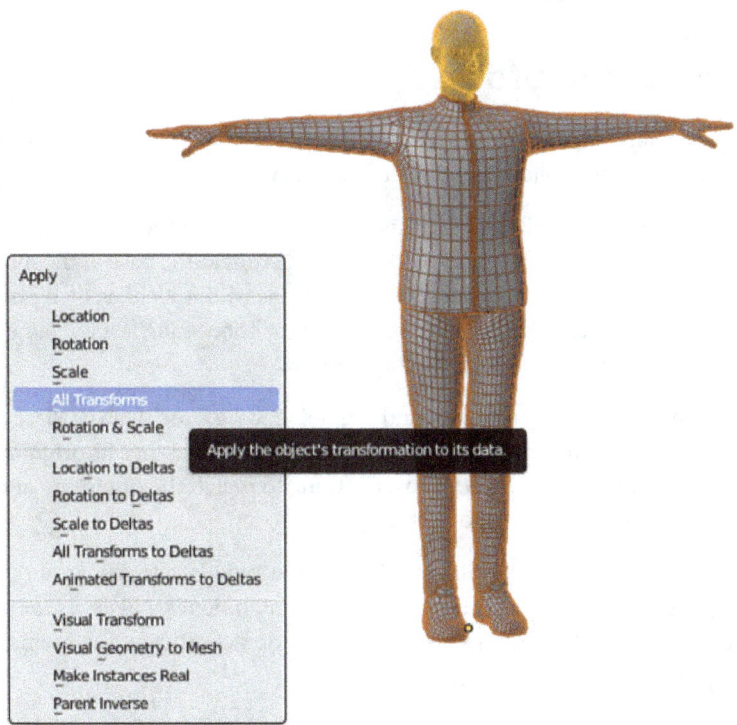

Figure 4.2 – Preparing objects

What this does is clear all stored transforms on models. Due to how Blender works, these transforms can be passed on and can influence other entities if used with constraints. This can cause all kinds of chaos. If you have made any changes to transforms and they are applied to the mesh, you will not lose any changes made. It just means that these changes will no longer interfere with any further work.

This moves the origin to the center of the scene, right between the feet of our model. It's also worth noting that you should apply select modifiers, if there are any; it all depends on how you plan on rigging. Models can come with subsurface and mirror modifiers. These and many other modifiers should work just fine. It doesn't need to be done as long as the armature modifier is below any others in the modifier stack.

With the model prepared, we can move on to rigging. Note that when you rig your own work, you most likely will need to fix/modify the mesh itself. This model has already been tested and optimized so there will be no need for further fixes.

We will add our armature here so that everything has the same origin point. This is a good practice as it will avoid some issues that can be hard to diagnose.

In this section, we have opened the model and prepared it for rigging by applying all of its transforms. With this done, we can move on to rigging.

Starting the rigging process

In this section, we will start the rigging process by placing an armature and entering **Edit Mode** to make our first move with bones, following up with areas such as the spine, arms, legs, and hands.

We begin with the root bone, typically placing this bone at the hips of the rig, or the center of mass for the object. Other times, you may be required to place the root at the base of the model between the feet; it just depends on the use case for your rig. If it remains within Blender, then placing the root bone at the hips will do just fine. It's common to place the root bone at the feet for game engines due to the way they work. We will cover a hip root setup for now.

Take exceptional caution when adding armature and beginning to rig. I ask that you place the armature object's origin in the center of the scene because the human model also has its origin in the center. *Matching the origins up is an absolute must.* It costs nothing to match the origins up and it will save you from all kinds of painful issues later down the line.

Using *Shift + A* to add an armature, we will enter **Edit Mode** and place this bone at the base of the spine/hips. The gap we leave between the tailbone and the thigh bones will act as the tailbone and hips; we don't need a separate bone for hips because the hips do not articulate and remain planted at the bottom of the spine.

> **Important note**
> Ensure your 3D cursor is placed at the world origin and that when you add your armature, it is added at the location shown in *Figure 4.3*. You can bring up the cursor snap menu with *Shift + S*:

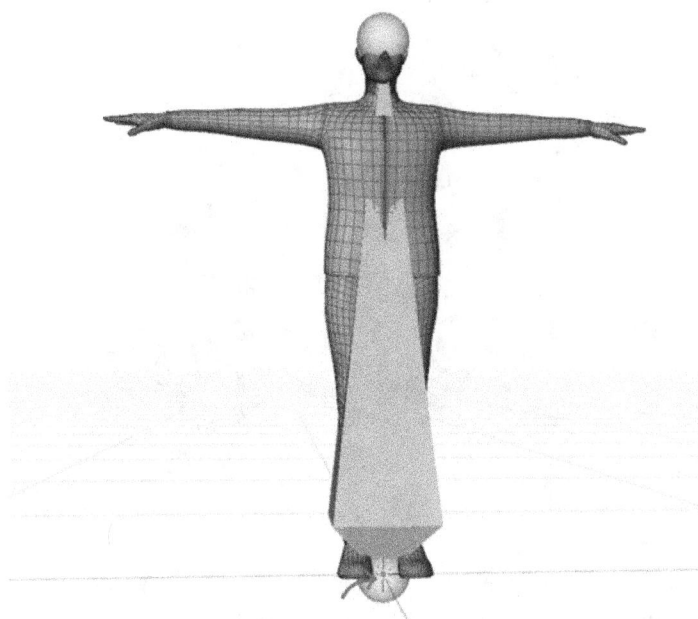

Figure 4.3 – Origin for all objects

With our armature in the scene, we can go into **Edit Mode** and begin building our rig. We will break this down into sections, starting with the spine.

Spine

Place the first bone at the bottom of the spine (this should be in the middle of the hips), and we will extrude out from it all the way up to the base of the neck.

As you should know, spines curve and twist. To facilitate this, we need multiple bones in a chain to make the spine.

The number of bones you place is entirely up to you; having fewer bones makes it easier to pose, while having more bones gives greater control (up to a point). I have placed four bones here as that should provide a good balance.

The root bone at the base of the spine chain is placed in the middle of the hips. The bones have a slight curve and end at the base of the neck. From the top of this chain, the neck will continue up and the shoulders will protrude out toward the arms:

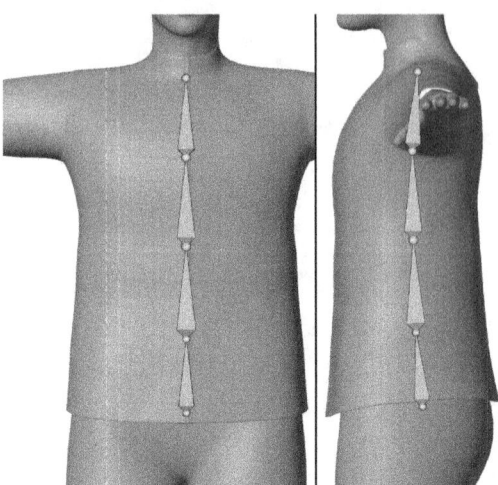

Figure 4.4 – Spine placed

The placement of bones within a volume will be discussed in more detail when we move to the hands. For now, however, we are placing the spine center of the torso volume.

To recap: We added an armature, making sure that the origin of the armature is in the center of the scene. Then, we used the root bone to form the basis of the spine, and we extruded upward along the model up to the neck. Now, let's move on to rigging the legs.

Legs

Moving on to the legs, we're going to start from the thigh, move through the knee to the ankle, and finish with the toes.

As we rig the legs, it may look as though we have no bone for the hips, but this is handled by the root bone. If you think about the dynamics of your own body, your hips follow the base of your spine: they're attached. So, we have no need to make a hip bone when we can just use the spine base. Let's get started with these steps:

1. Duplicate the first bone in the spine (the root bone) and place it where you expect the thigh bone to be. My inputs go as follows: *Shift + D* (duplicate), *G* (grab, placing the base of the new bone at the top of the thigh), select the tip, press *G* and then *Z*, and drag down to the knee.

    Remember to move to the side orthographic view every so often (*Alt + MMB*) to place the bone inside the leg.

    We're aiming to place the bone more toward the rear. Look at *Figure 4.4* for exactly where I placed my bones.

2. Select this thigh bone and *Shift + LMB* the base of the spine. Press *Ctrl + P* to open the parenting menu and select **Keep Offset**. This keeps the legs connected to the rest of the body without a bone to hold the distance. This is what the hip does, but that's a waste of a bone if we can just use an offset relationship instead.

3. Extrude this down to form the shin. Remember to pan your view and use the orthographic view to get things lined up in a more precise manner. Head down to the ankle with this bone, landing as squarely in the middle of the ankle as you can. From here, go into the side view as the front view isn't very useful for our next move.

4. Extrude again to form the foot, going straight from the ankle down to the base of the toes. While the example model doesn't have toes, we still need a toe bend bone for the shoe; otherwise, the foot will be a big stiff brick. Check *Figure 4.5* for a good place to end this bone.

5. Finish the leg chain with a toe bone, otherwise referred to as a **foot peel** bone or foot bend bone. Make sure the foot bone follows the foot not just from the side view but also the front and even top view. The feet on this model point outward slightly. Follow this with the foot bones.

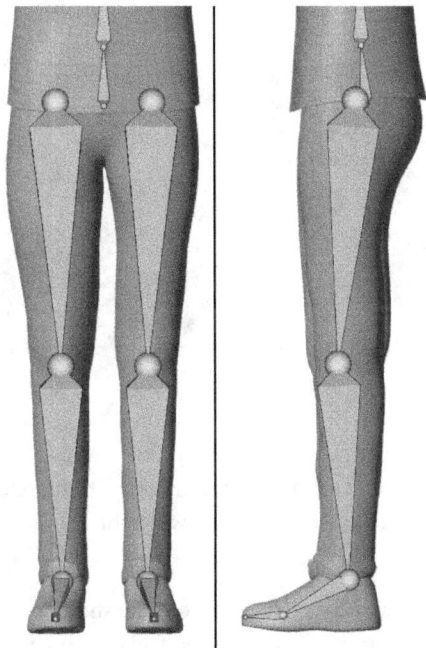

Figure 4.5 – Left leg chain

Don't worry about the other leg; we have a tool to mirror the entire rig that we will be using when we reach the *Naming and mirroring* section later in this chapter. If you ever have the opportunity to mirror your work, then do so. It halves your workload and, more often than not, the model will be mirrored, so it makes everything neat and pleasant on the eye to have a symmetrical rig.

Arms

Moving on to the arms, the process is almost identical to the legs. In fact, what we did with the legs and spine is pretty much the basis of building a rig. The only notable difference is the hands and fingers.

Fingers can be the cause of some pain. They're hard to get right as our visibility is limited, but more on that when we get to it.

Start by extruding from the top of the spine. This bone will be the shoulder. Unlike the legs, we want to keep this bone connected to the spine:

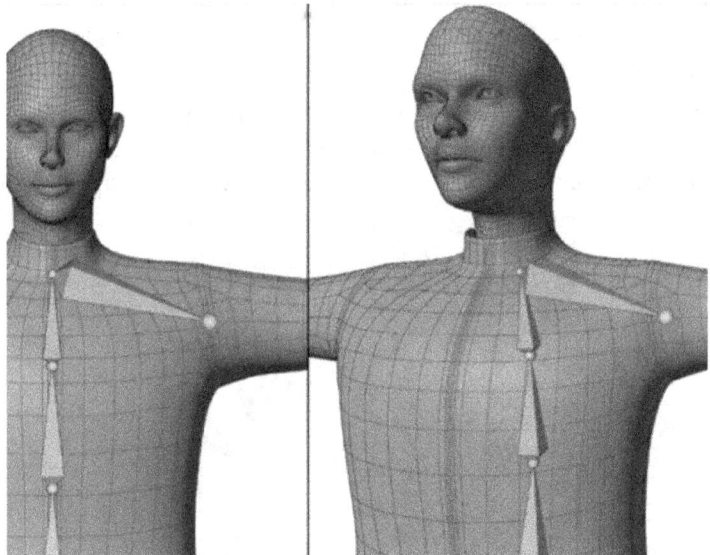

Figure 4.6 – Shoulder

Next, we need to make the upper and lower arm. Usually, this is a case of extruding from the shoulder to the elbow, and then from the elbow to the wrist. However, it's not clear where the elbow on this model is, so we're going to assume it's in the middle between the shoulder and the wrist, as is the case for our own bodies.

We can get the exact middle of the arm by extruding from the shoulder straight to the wrist and then subdividing the bone. A subdivision splits the bone in half, giving us a joint in the middle, right where we want our elbow to be.

Subdividing bones

To start subdividing the bones, follow these steps:

1. Start by extruding from the shoulder to the wrist:

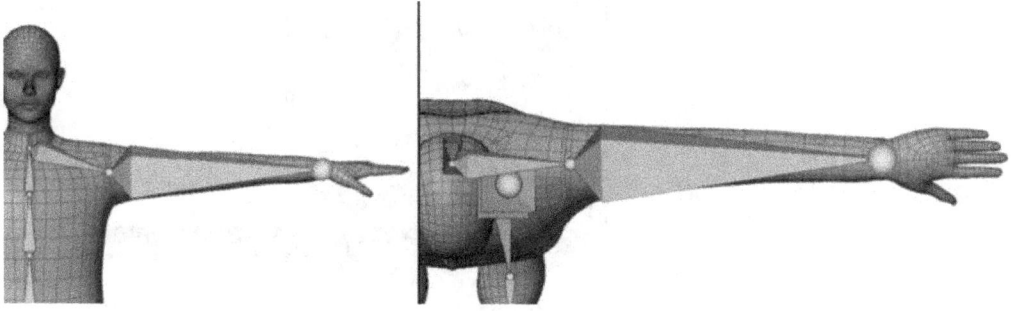

Figure 4.7 – Shoulder-to-wrist extrusion

2. Next, select the body of the bone and press *F3*; this will bring up the search box.

> **Tip**
> The search box is an exceptionally powerful tool. You can find pretty much anything in it. If you know what you want but can't find it, search for it.

3. Type Subdivide, and an option called **Armature | Subdivide** should appear. Click on it and your arm bone will be subdivided into two. Alternatively, you can find this option in the **Armature** menu pictured in *Figure 4.8*:

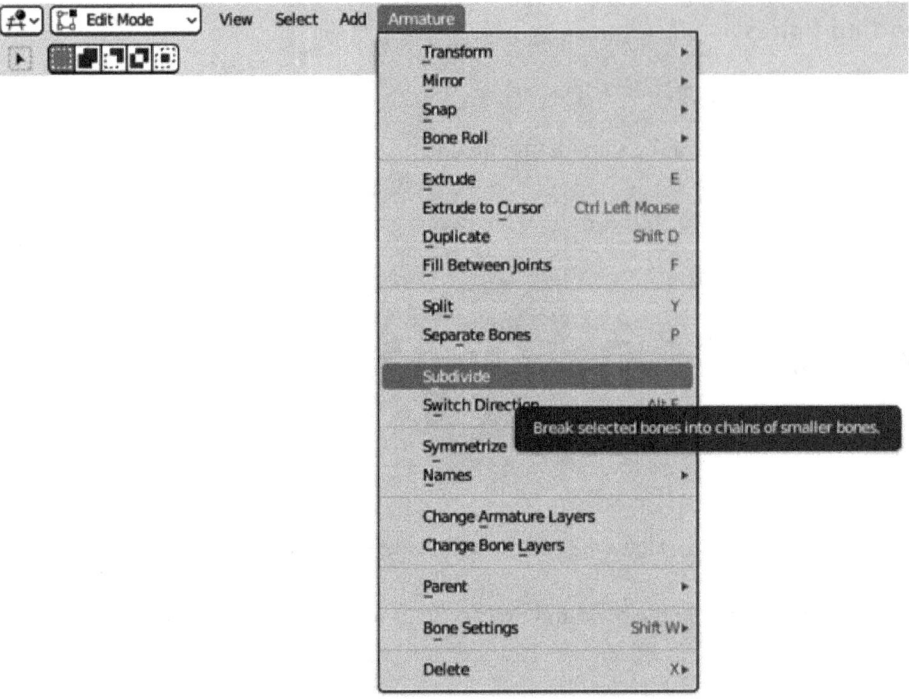

Figure 4.8 – Subdivide menu option

4. After subdividing the arm bone, grab each joint in the arm and place them in the center of the arm, making sure to take all viewpoints into account.

    Here is an image of my arm. You might notice the bones have some odd rotation or *bone roll*. We will learn more about this when we do the fingers.

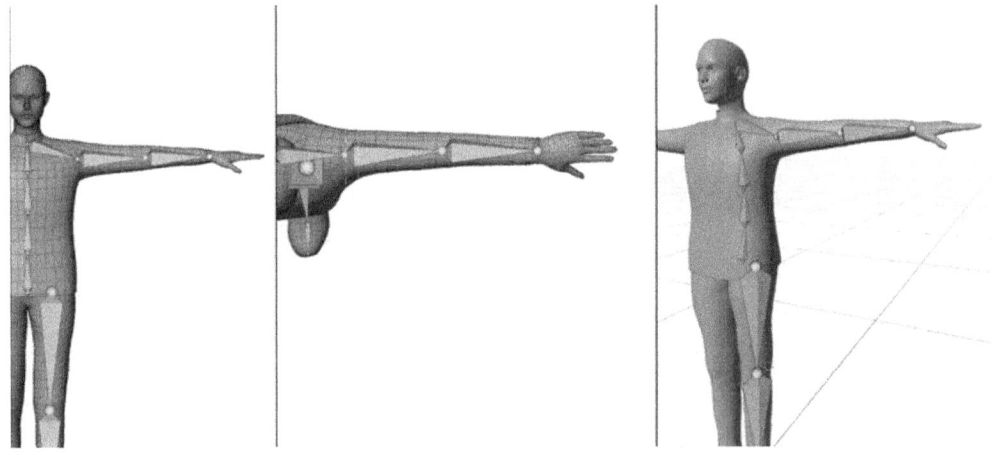

Figure 4.9 – Arm bones placed

To recap: We have used chains of bones to build the spine and arms. This is one of the cores of rigging. Hands are up next; they can be the most tedious part of rigging due to how small each finger is and their proximity to one another.

Hands

Hands will be a real test of competence; they demand a substantial amount of your time when compared to the rest of the rig.

There's an impressive snapping mode called **Snap To | Volume**. This can make fingers an absolute breeze. To explain exactly how it works would be pointless. Instead, *Figure 4.10* shows you the setting you will most commonly use with this tool. Copy *Figure 4.10* and start grabbing joints to see how they center themselves inside the fingers. I have written the rest of this section without using this tool as that is my personal preference, but make sure you give it a try as it can save you a lot of time.

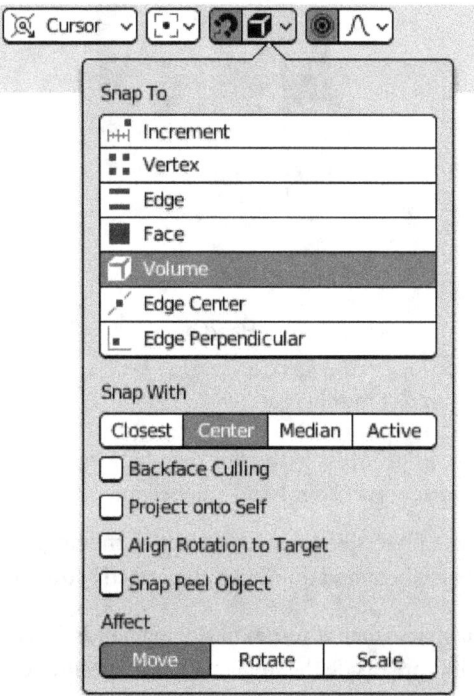

Figure 4.10 – Snapping tool settings

Start with a top-down orthographic view of the hand. Extrude and duplicate until your bones look something like *Figure 4.11*. Don't stress about getting it perfect; you can iterate and modify a rig even after it's fully finished.

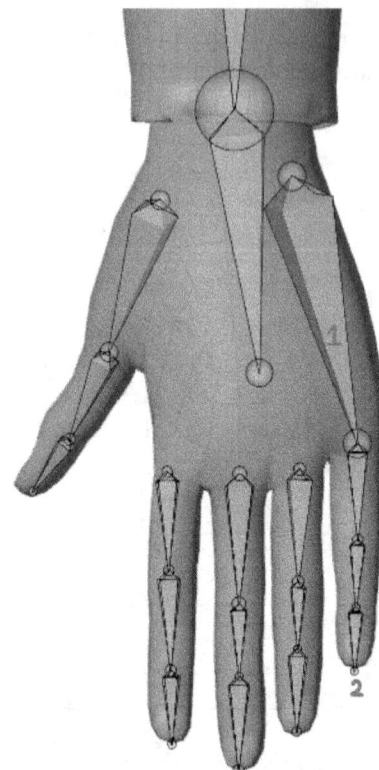

Figure 4.11 – Hand bones

Figure 4.11 has some points of interest numbered:

- **Point 1**: This is a squeeze bone. Mess with your own hands and you will notice that you can grip across your hand and squeeze. Your hand will become narrower; this bone does just that.
- **Point 2**: The bones for the fingers end just at the tips of the fingers, with the chain following the fingers. If the fingers are bent and do not track perfectly straight, then so must the bones.

There are many, many different styles when it comes to rigging hands. This is just my personal choice. Also, take note of where the joints are inside the fingers. There's specific geometry put in place to give good deformation to the fingers. You'll notice the same three loop joints in most fingers you come across. Try and place the joints on the main loop as shown in *Figure 4.12*:

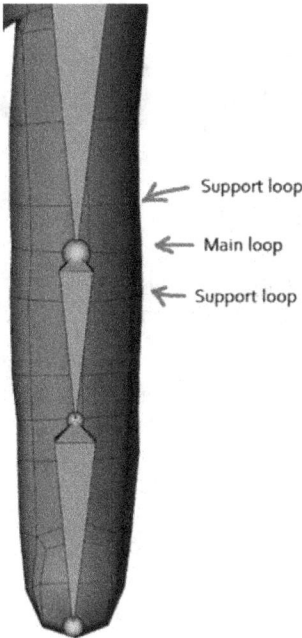

Support loop

Main loop

Support loop

Figure 4.12 – Finger loops

We have aligned the bones from the top, but what about the sides? You can go ahead and try to align them by just changing to the front view, but it's going to be a cluttered mess. It would be much easier if we could hide all the bones we don't want and just work on one finger at a time.

Here is how:

1. Select all bones we want to work on; we will hide all the bones that are unselected.

2. Press *Shift + H*; this is an inverse hide. It will hide unselected bones and leave our selected bones in place.

3. Once finished you can press *Alt + H* to unhide everything.

4. Go ahead and select all the bones in the index finger. Press *Shift + H* and enter the front orthographic view.

5. Grab each joint and get them into position; look at *Figure 4.13* for guidance. Notice where the joints are placed and how the bones remain in the middle of the fingers. Placing the bone further toward the surface will produce better results on said surface but consequently produce worse results underneath (and vice versa).

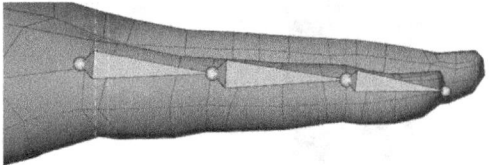

Figure 4.13 – Finger joints placed

If we are too low on the joints then the knuckles will bulge out; if we are too high, then the inside of the fingers will intersect heavily when the hand is closed.

Again, placing the bone further toward the surface will produce better results on said surface but consequently produce worse results underneath (and vice versa). *Figure 4.12* shows the bones placed near the top because the outside of the hand will be far more visible than the inside when the fingers are closed. Therefore, I do not need to worry so much about the inside. Your needs may vary.

6. Now press *Alt + H*, select the next finger, and go again.

> **Tip**
> You can switch to wireframe mode to see through the fingers.

It can be hard to get the bones in a good place when it comes to the fingers, but take your time and remember that you can come back and adjust as you please.

7. Even more difficult is the thumb. Due to the angle the thumb has been made at, orthographic views won't work well. You will need to pan your view around. Again, placing the bone further toward the surface will produce better results on said surface but consequently produce worse results underneath (and vice versa).

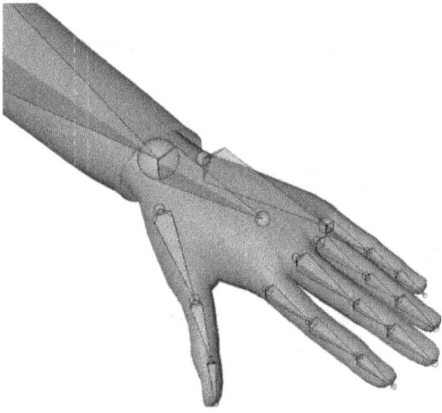

Figure 4.14 – Example hand

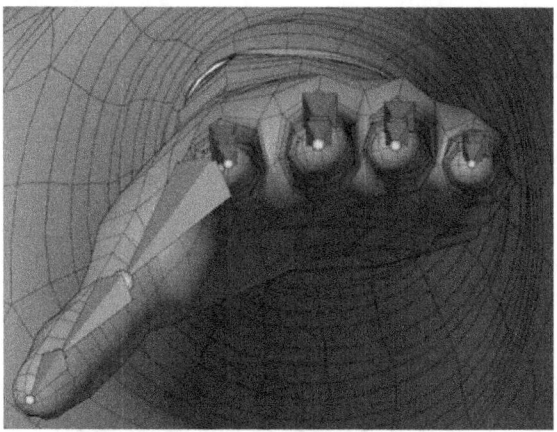

Figure 4.15 – Another view of the example hand

When you feel like you have finished, we can move on to the neck. Remember, you can always come back and add touchups at any stage.

Neck and head

There shouldn't be any need to explain this step by step. Extrude from the neck and get something similar to *Figure 4.16*:

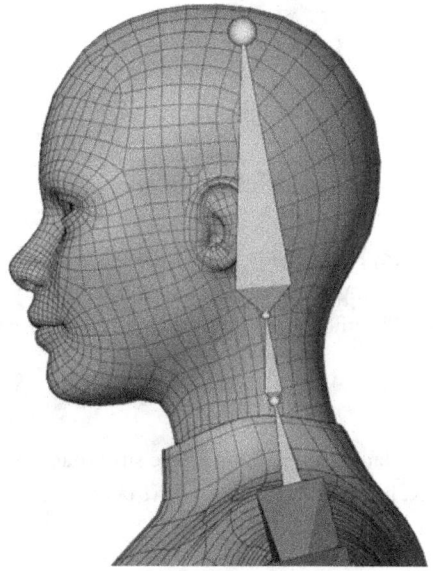

Figure 4.16 – Neck and head

We're not going to cover the face in this book as that is not within the scope of an introduction. Zooming out, you should have an armature somewhat similar to *Figure 4.17*. We're going to name and mirror all these bones next.

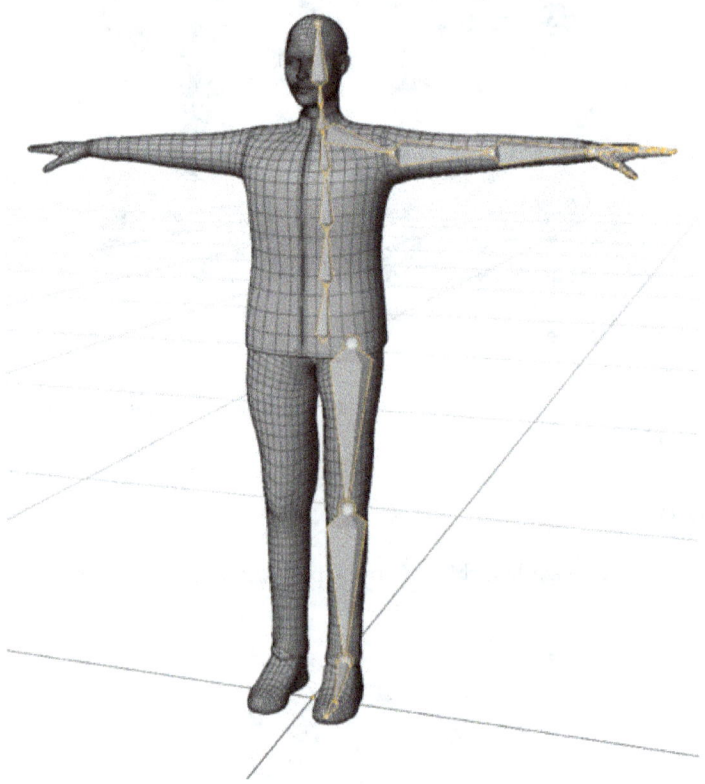

Figure 4.17 – Half a rig

We have placed all the bones needed. For the side that's missing, we will mirror it when we get to the *Naming and mirroring* section. Mirroring is a final step and should only be done when we are sure that our bones are finalized. There are still some issues that need addressing; we will fix these as we progress.

Bone roll

Now that all the bones have been placed, we need to make sure that they have the correct bone roll. It's important for both IK and FK, but mostly FK. It doesn't take long to fix and will add quality and ease of use to your rig.

As mentioned earlier in *Figure 1.3 from Chapter 1,* under the *Bone Transforms* sub-heading, bones can roll. This is important as when they roll, their axis follows. If the roll is wrong when it comes to posing and animating, the whole rig will fall apart.

You may notice on your rig that some bones do not have an expected roll.

In *Figure 4.18,* you can see that the arm of the mesh is perfectly horizontal, and if the elbow were to bend, we would expect it to bend along a horizontal plane. However, in this figure, you can see that the bone roll would not give the expected results. If we want the expected results, we should align the bone with the red arrow shown in the figure.

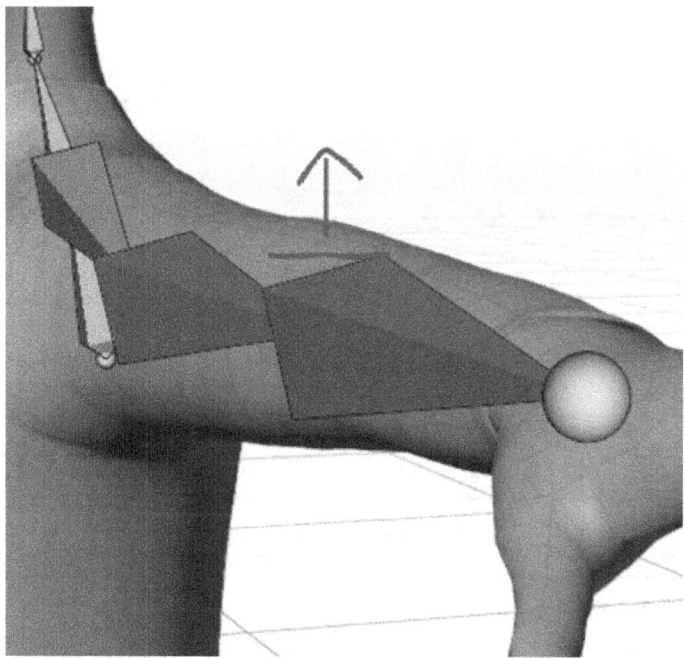

Figure 4.18 – Hand names

In *Figure 4.18,* you can see how the bones in the arm don't have the expected roll (the expected is drawn in red) and we need to fix this. In *Figure 4.19,* you can also see how the axes are completely different. If an animator were to input R (*for rotate*) + Z (*Selecting the Z axis*) to rotate around the Z axis, they would get wildly different results from these bones:

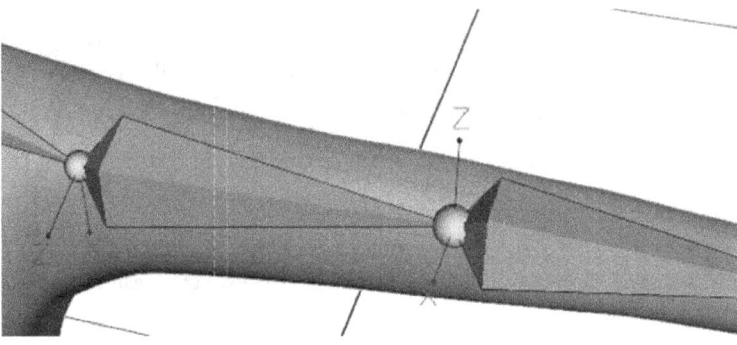

Figure 4.19 – Hand names

The upper arm bone would rotate up and down while the lower arm bone would rotate horizontally, which is mildly infuriating, to say the least. See the option highlighted in *Figure 4.19* to show these axes for yourself.

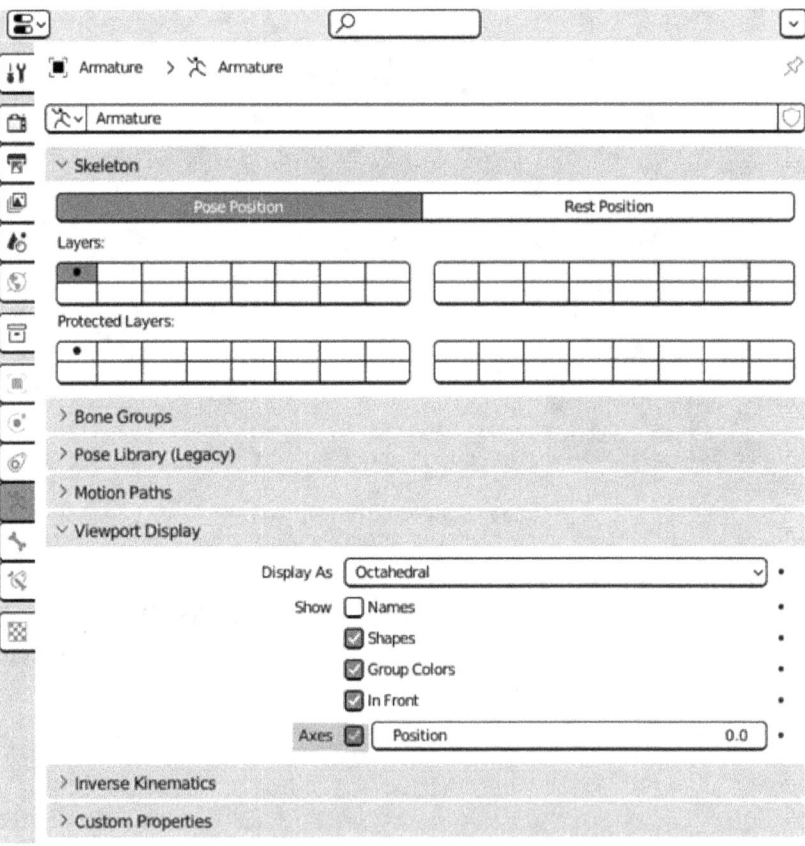

Figure 4.20 – Show bone axes

When you find that a chain of bones has suboptimal roll, you can use the **Recalculate Roll** menu:

1. Select all the bones that need correcting *in the same direction*. Do not select feet and fingers as their rolls will be different.

2. Press *Shift + N* to open the **Recalculate Roll** menu. There are plenty of options here and I suggest you give them all a read. They're all pretty useful (especially the cursor one: it spins bones to face your 3D cursor).

3. We're going to use **Global + Z Axis** as it will result in our bones facing up in the Z axis, and that's ideal for our arms here.

To recap: We have added the needed bones on one side. Whenever you can, you should always make half and mirror. We do this because it halves the amount of work we need to do and ensures that what we make is perfectly symmetrical. In some instances, symmetry might not be ideal, but in such cases, you can still mirror the rig and then make adjustments. We also made final tweaks to the bone roll to ensure that the rig performs well and has consistent transforms throughout.

Now we will get on to mirroring and naming. Naming must follow a structure, and naming bones before mirroring reduces the workload significantly.

Naming and mirroring

In this section, we will be naming our bones using the **Bone Properties** tab and the correct naming standards. We will also be mirroring our rig with **Symmetrize** to finish the rigging process.

Naming can be very important depending on what kind of pipeline you are a part of. Motion capture and game engine exporting are two key instances where you really should name the bones in your rig. Renaming bones makes it easier to find them in the hierarchy and when typing in names to quickly set up constraints. It's a quality-of-life improvement that should always be made when possible.

Rigs should follow a naming scheme that makes sense. Names must be specific to their bones: not `Arm.001` and `Arm.002` but instead `UpperArm` and `LowerArm`.

For humanoid characters, this is easy, but you may find that you're rigging something that's far from humanoid. If that's the case, try to keep your naming short and readable, keeping in mind that your rig may pass into the hands of many people who will be grateful if your naming makes sense.

Bones that will be mirrored (bones that are in the middle, such as the spine, will not be mirrored) need to have a side suffix added for both clarity and for Blender's mirroring tool to work correctly. A naming suffix can look like **Bone_L**, **Bone.L**, **Bone.Right**, and so on. What you choose is down to personal preference, but for now, we will use **Bone.L**.

Renaming bones

The process for renaming bones is as follows:

1. Enter **Edit Mode** with the armature selected.

2. Select the bone you want to rename.

3. Head over to the **Bone Properties** tab:

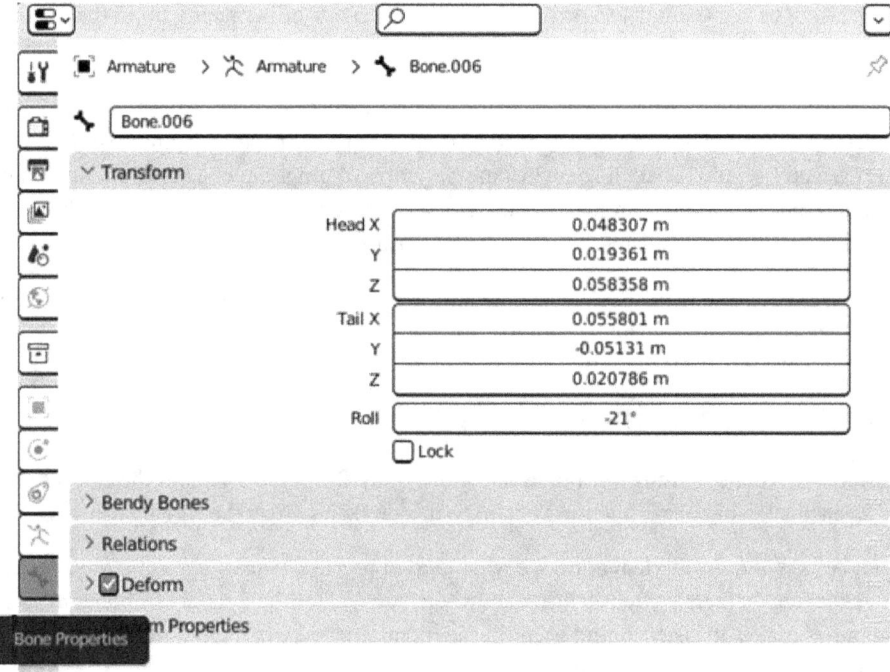

Figure 4.21 – Bone name field

4. You will see the bone name at the top of this menu (**Bone.006** in this figure). Go ahead and double-click this field to edit the name of the bone. You can use this field to rename any other object in the scene too; it's good practice to do so. The following figures show examples of the named bones.

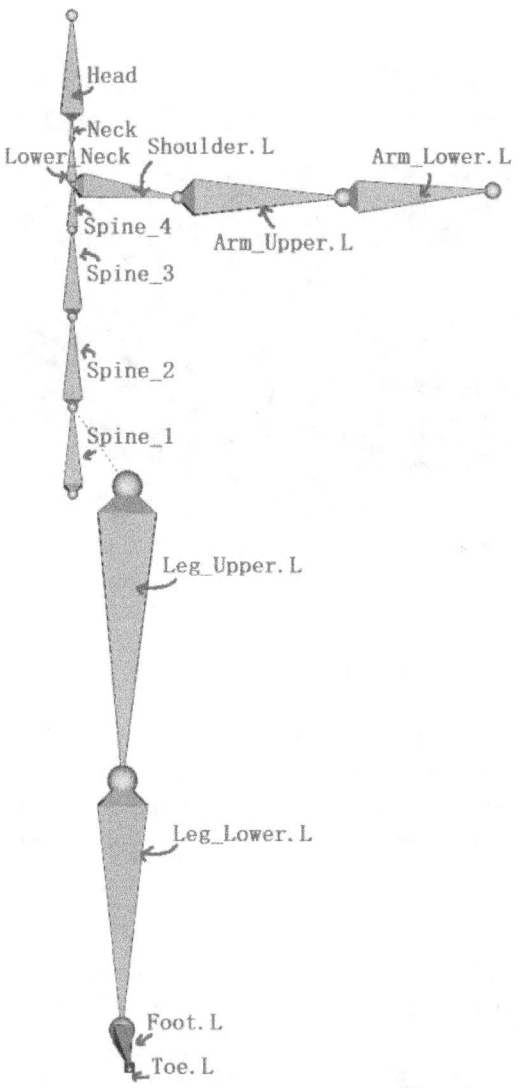

Figure 4.22 – Rig names

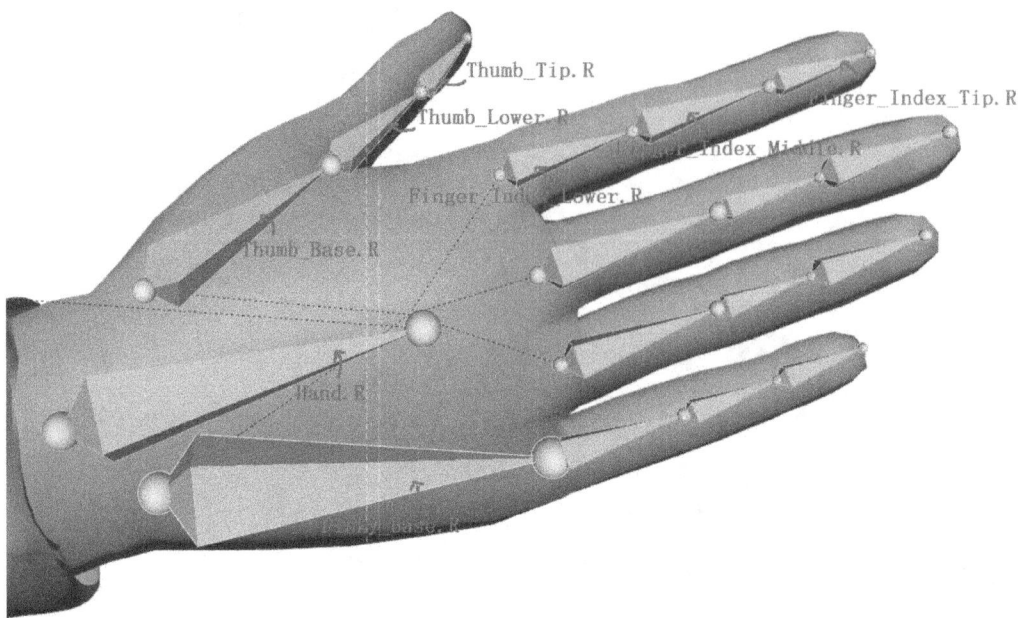

Figure 4.23 – Hand names

Figure 4.22 and *Figure 4.23* show the names I have given to my bones. They're named in such a way that searching for them by name should be stress-free, although you don't need to worry too much about names as it may only be you interacting with the rig at this kind of level. With naming out of the way, we can perform the final step in the rig creation process: mirroring our work.

Mirroring

We use mirroring in our work whenever possible to directly halve the work required. The less time it takes to get your result the better. The ability to cut repetition and tedium out of your work is a clear sign of efficiency and skill.

To finish the rig, we need to mirror it. To start the mirroring process, follow these steps:

1. Select the armature and enter **Edit Mode**.

2. Select all the bones we want to mirror. This will be any bone that does not lie in the middle, such as arms and legs – don't forget the shoulder.

3. Click **Armature | Symmetrize**:

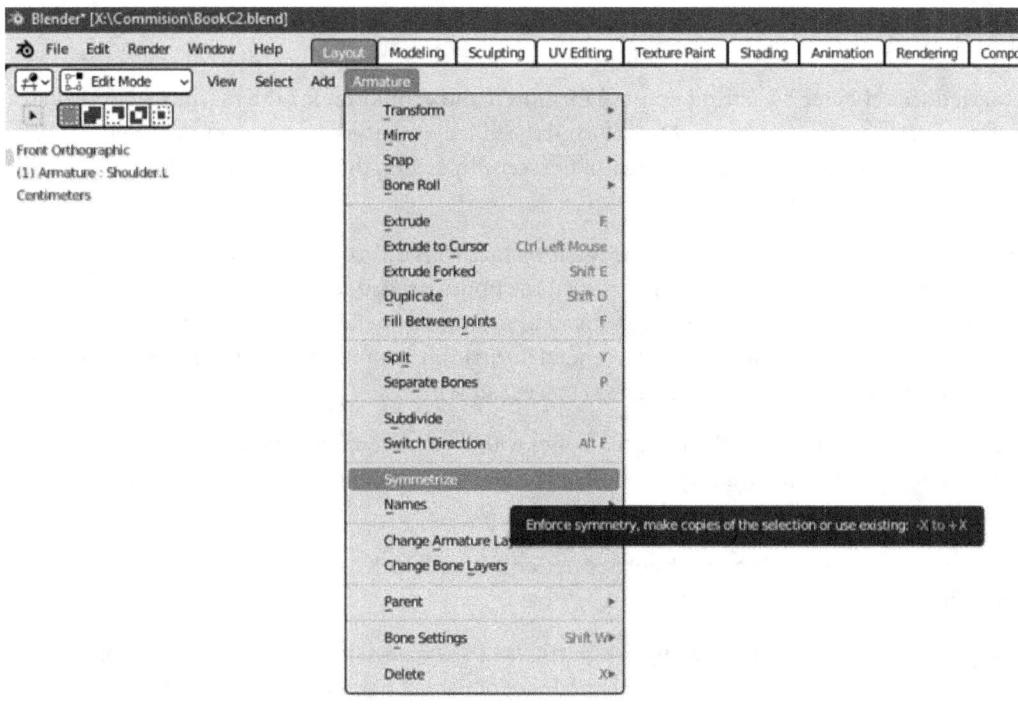

Figure 4.24 – The Symmetrize option

If all goes well, you will have a mirrored rig, with all the new bones carrying identical names but with a **Bone.R** suffix.

We named our bones before mirroring because the mirror automatically flips the names, hence the need to adhere to the naming conventions. If we don't name the bones correctly, then Blender would be unable to automatically give the new bones the correct suffix.

Summary

We started this chapter by setting up both our mesh and armature; for the mesh, we applied all transforms using *Ctrl + A* to prevent transform-related issues that are very common in rigging. We also set the origin of the mesh to the center of the scene by setting the transforms so that we can add an armature in the same place.

Moving on to bones, we made sure to place an armature with the same origin location as the mesh. With the armature set up, we went on to add all the bones needed to get the desired deformation, placing the bones closest to surfaces that demand more accurate deformation and further away from surfaces that are of little concern to the overall deformation (comparing the visible outside of the fingers to the obscured inside of the fingers is one example).

We then learned how to correctly name the bones with a consistent naming scheme, using suffixes such as .L or _L and names that represent the bone location to denote to Blender and any end users what each bone is and where it is.

To finish our work, we used the **Symmetrize** option with all the left-hand bones selected to mirror them to the opposite side.

That concludes the bone part of rigging; we're halfway to a finished product. In the next chapter, we will be weight painting. You already have experience of weight painting, but now we're going to do it on a much larger scale.

5

Getting Started with Weight Painting

In the previous chapter, we started setting up a model and adding an **armature**, and then we placed all the necessary bones inside the model and named all the bones.

In this chapter, we will cover weight painting, the second half of the process of bringing a mesh to life. We already touched on the basics in *Chapter 3*, but now, we will move on to applying more advanced thinking to more complex problems. We will run into issues such as creasing and stretching, so we will learn to overcome them with careful attention to both weights and bone placement. This will help us to produce a result that is both pleasing in performance and can produce expected results.

We will move from limb to limb, discovering the unique problems each can bring, and see how we can mitigate/eliminate these issues.

In this chapter, we will cover the following topics:

- Setting up empty weights
- Rigging the feet
- Understanding mesh seams and overlaps
- Rigging the knee
- Rigging the hips

By the end of this chapter, you will be able to apply weights to any mesh to achieve good, predictable deformation, recognizing common issues and understanding their causes and respective solutions.

Setting up empty weights

To get started, let's set up some empty weights. Use **Armature Deform | With Empty Groups**, as this option generates groups with empty weights. If we leave the weights up to Blender by choosing the default options, we are guaranteed to have to clean up a frustrating mess.

We will start by parenting the mesh to the rig we have just made, and then we will enter Weight Paint Mode. If you have forgotten how exactly to do this, here's a quick series of steps as a reminder:

1. In **Object Mode**, select all the meshes (head, body, hands, feet).

2. Staying in Object Mode, press *Shift* to select the armature.

3. Press *Ctrl + P* to open the parenting menu, and select **Armature Deform | With Empty Groups**.

    You can verify this has worked by grabbing the armature and dragging it around; all the mesh will follow. If any mesh doesn't follow, you can just select said meshes and parent them on their own, and they will be added.

4. If for some reason this doesn't work, you might get some errors such as **loop in parents**; if so, just select all the objects that you are parenting (In this case all the meshes that make up the character), press *Alt + P*, select **Clear parent** and then start again.

5. Deselect everything with *A*, and then select the armature. We will start with the feet, so press *Shift* to select the feet, and then enter **Weight Paint** mode:

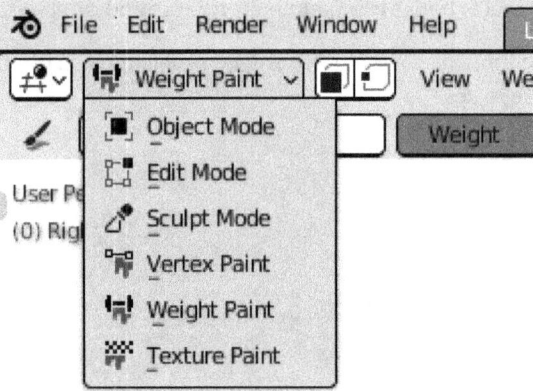

Figure 5.1 – Weight Paint Mode

6. If all has gone well, the shoe will be blue, and you will be able to select the bones in the rig. Just like how we weight-painted in *Chapter 3*, select the bone before you paint and adjust your brush settings accordingly.

7. Remember that the shoe is selected. Press / on your number pad to enter local view; this hides everything apart from what we have selected. You can exit this mode by pressing / again (going back into global view).

Here's a quick recap:

1. Select all the meshes.

2. Select the armature.

3. Click *Ctrl + P*, and parent with the **empty vertex groups**.

4. Select the armature (this will deselect all the meshes), then select the mesh you want to weight paint, and enter Weight Paint Mode.

5. Use / to enter local view.

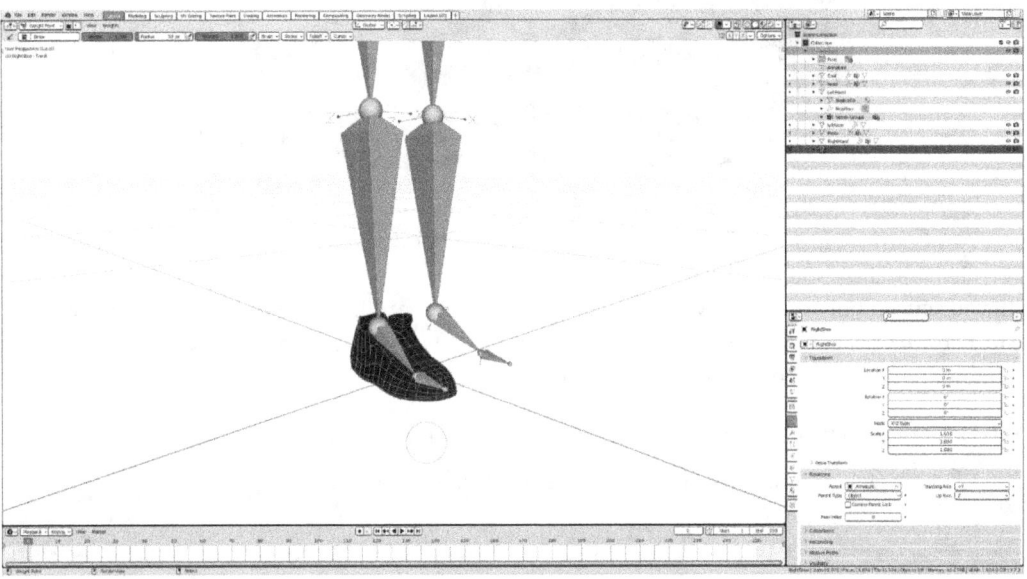

Figure 5.2 – Beginning weight painting

Your screen should look like this, with the blue mesh representing weights of 0 (empty), a new cursor in a circle to represent our brush, and the bones selectable.

With that done, we can begin painting weights. I'm going to show you how I painted the weights for each bone and mesh, pointing out anything that is of key importance. Let's get started!

Rigging the feet

You should already know the process for painting weights, but here it is again:

1. As we did in the previous section, select the correct bones and mesh in weight paint mode.

2. Set the weight and strength of the default brush you have to a desired amount (1.0 will do for now).

3. Hold and left-click over the mesh to begin painting weights onto it.

By following these steps, you should have something that looks like this:

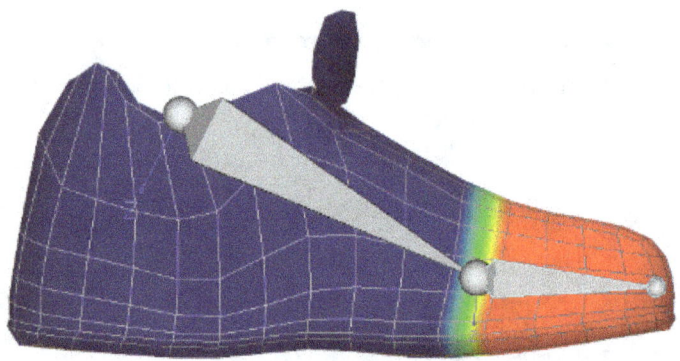

Figure 5.3 – Initial toe weights

With your current brush, Draw, you will see that you paint hard lines; there's a Blur brush we can use to give softer edges once we have laid down our weights. The Blur tool is great for making soft transitions between two bones; here is how to find it:

1. Head to the left-hand side of Blender to find a small gray pull tab.

2. Click this tab to reveal brushes you can use in Weight Paint Mode:

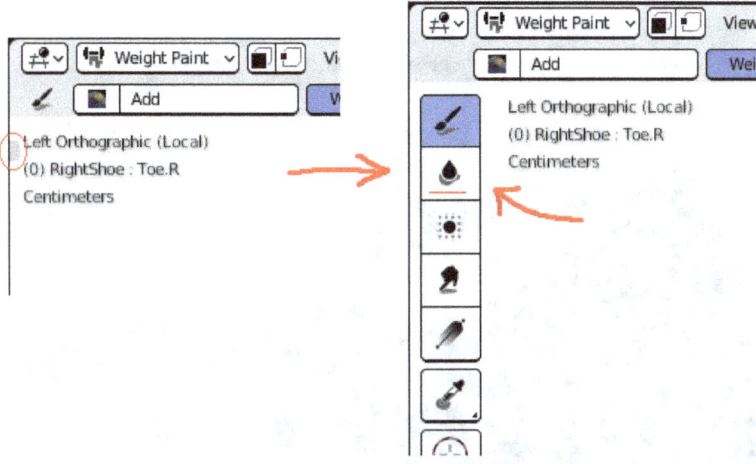

Figure 5.4 – Finding the Blur tool

Starting with a solid color, I will place my gradient on the joint between the toe bone and the foot bone, as this is where the shoe will flex. I run the cursor over the gradient while holding left-click to average the weights under the brush.

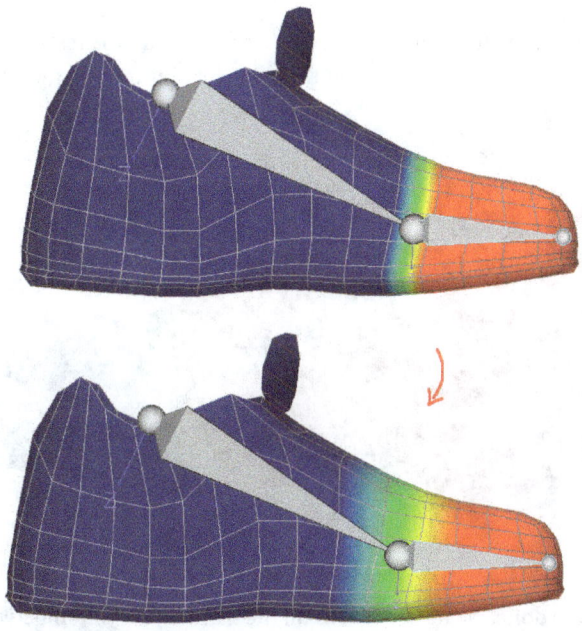

Figure 5.5 – The Blur tool effect

This is how my toe has ended up looking, after brushing over the gradient with the Blur tool. As long as you add your weights to this approximate area, it should work. The geometry is quite simple here:

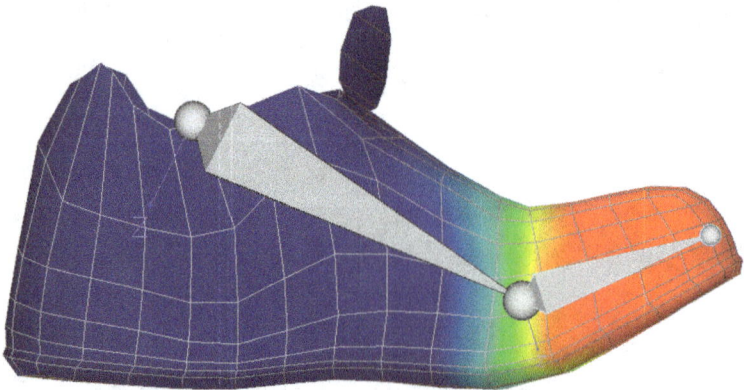

Figure 5.6 – Toe weights

After finishing weights on each bone, we should check the deformation; however, we can't really check the deformation yet, as the rest of the foot has no weights yet, so let's fix that.

Repeating the steps you just took to paint the toes, go ahead and paint the rest of the foot. Use the Paint tool to set the rest of the foot to a weight of 1, and then use the Blur tool to smoothen out the gradient.

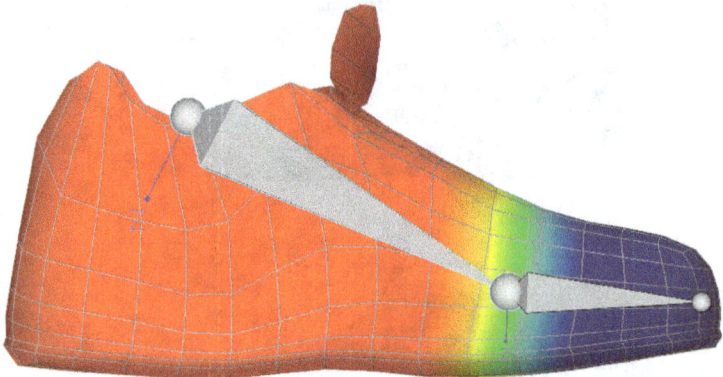

Figure 5.7 – The foot weights

Once both toe and foot are done, we need to focus on the handoff/transition between them and make sure it looks as we expect. The foot is super simple, so it makes a great place to establish the basic skills we will continue throughout this work.

Select the toe bone, press *R* to rotate it, and push the toes up by a reasonable amount; don't overdo it. As you can see in *Figure 5.8*, there's a dip on top of the joint that shouldn't be there; this is because the control area for the toes does not extend far enough up the shoe.

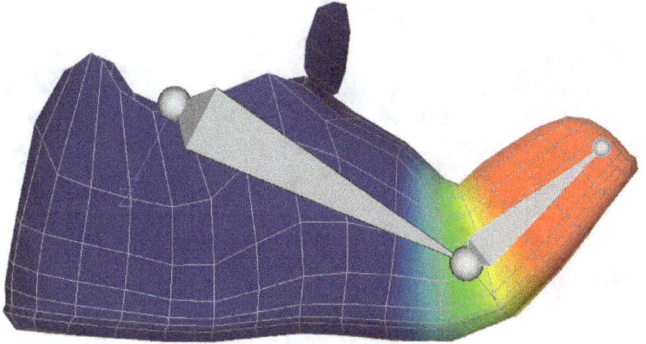

Figure 5.8 – Stressing to find issues

Subtracting can leave holes in the weights; if we subtract the foot weights, nothing will be there to replace it.

So instead, select the toe bone and place some light weight (~0.2) further up the foot. You can do this by adjusting the weight of the current paint tool (see *Figure 3.11 – Weight paintbrush options* in *Chapter 3* for a reminder).

We essentially push the weights from the toe up the face of the foot to make a more gradual transition. It's marked in Figure 5.9 with a red arrow showing the toe weights creeping up the front of the foot a little.

Here's how both of my bones look:

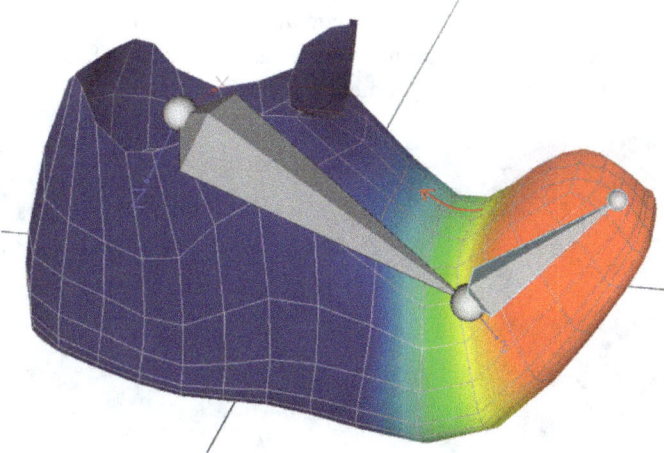

Figure 5.9 – The toe weights

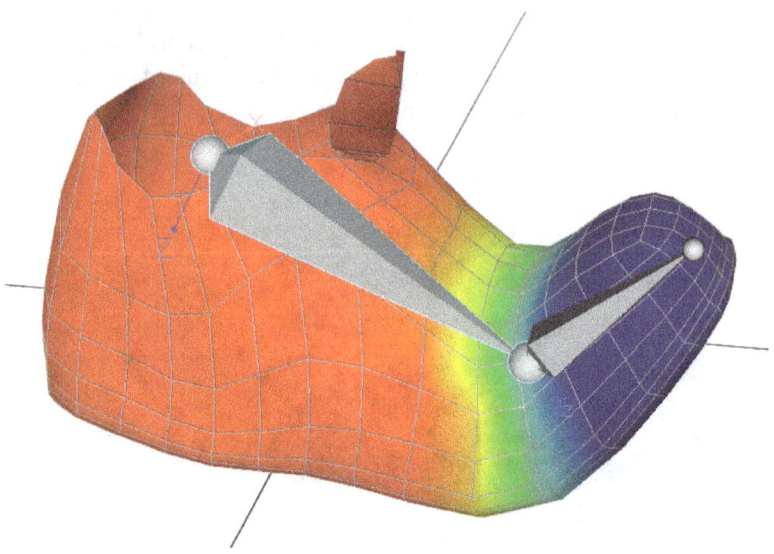

Figure 5.10 – The foot weights

Note how in *Figure 5.9*, the toe weights creep up the laces, and in *Figure 5.10*, the foot weights on the laces recede. This smooths that top transition and removes the dip issue we had in *Figure 5.8*. Grab the toe bones, flex them on your own work, and see how well it works.

That's the first weight painting milestone hit; next up are the legs (along with a little bit more theory). Feel free to polish your work at any point before moving on.

Understanding mesh seams and overlaps

Before we start weight painting our legs, it's important to discuss how models are made, their topology, and geometry. More specifically, we will examine mesh seams and overlaps. Take a look at *Figure 5.11*, which shows two different ways of merging geometry:

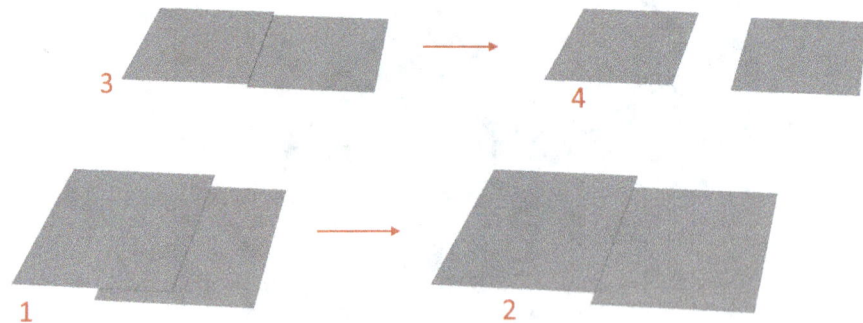

Figure 5.11 – Mesh overlaps

You can imagine the planes shown in *Figure 5.11* as two parts of a model. An artist has decided the vertices should not be connected. There are a number of reasons for doing this, such as the following:

- **Tech/engine limitations**: Some engines (mostly real-time game engines) of significant age have limitations with how they can display materials and textures. Separating meshes allows artists to treat different parts completely differently. This should only apply to old tech; hopefully, you will not have to deal with anything similar.

- **Artistic**: Another instance where you may find geometry like this is if certain parts are intended to be swapped out, so they cannot be joined together. Maybe this character can change their shoes or put on gloves; more often than not, this is achieved by simply swapping out the respective mesh.

In *Figure 5.11*, on the left is a mesh in its resting pose, and on the right is a mesh stretched out. The quadrants marked **1** and **2** show a mesh that has an overlap at rest. Quadrants **3** and **4** show a mesh without any overlap at rest. Quadrants **1** and **2** show the ideal way to create a mesh if there must be a break and the meshes cannot be joined together.

Note that when **3** is stretched to **4**, it shows a massive gap. The overlapping mesh that can be seen in example **1** avoids this by adding an overlap at rest so that when it is stretched out to position **2**, it will be able to achieve greater range before cracking. Note that overlapping is not immune to splitting; it just delays it by however much we need to achieve the intended range of motion.

With an overlap, there's less chance of a crack appearing in the mesh. However, you introduce a chance of mesh clipping, where the inside mesh pops out. On a single bone, this is not a problem, as there is no joint, but when a mesh overlaps over a joint (as shown in *Figure 5.12*), you must take extra care. The inner mesh could pierce the outer mesh if their weights do not match.

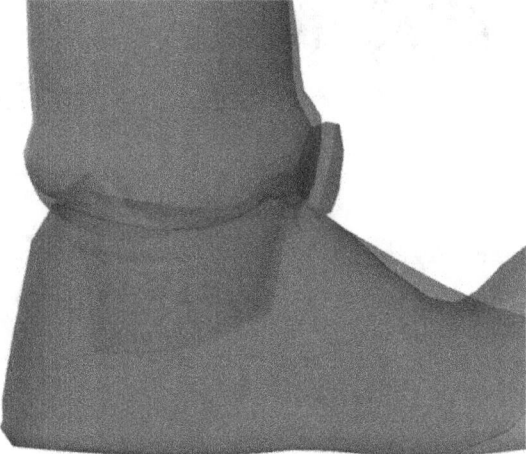

Figure 5.12 – A mesh overlap for the ankles

We want the weight handoff to be right on the joint. We should avoid giving the top of the foot any flex, as that would be unrealistic; instead, give the pants right above it the flex needed to manipulate the foot. If that confuses you, then take note the next time you put a pair of shoes on; you will find that it is your pants or even your socks that deform, not the shoe.

> **Important note**
>
> Remember that you need to go back into Object Mode and select the **bone and then the mesh**.

Figure 5.13 and *Figure 5.14* show how you should paint the weights. Take note of what bone is selected (highlighted in blue) in each diagram:

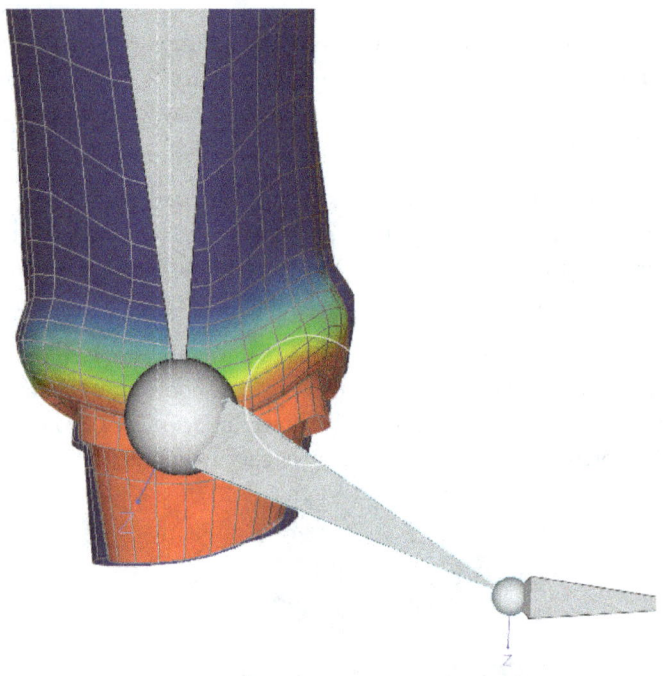

Figure 5.13 – Foot bone weights distorting the lower leg

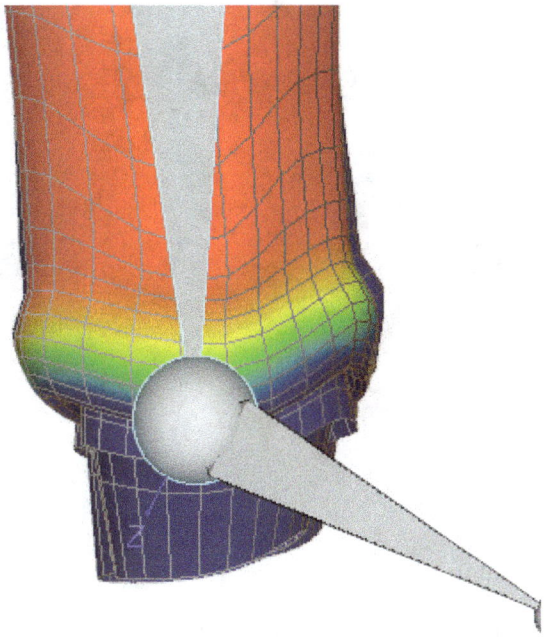

Figure 5.14 – Leg bone weights

For the leg bone, I used the shoe as a makeshift mask. Keep the shoe visible. Painting the leg above it will place your weight handoff in the correct place. Then, go ahead and smoothen it out a little with the **Blur** brush.

> **Important note**
> Remember that to hide a mesh (*H*) and show a mesh (*Alt + H*), you must be in Object Mode.

After painting the foot and leg, go ahead and stress-test your work. Select the foot bone, and rotate it into some random positions to see how the deformation works.

Note that if you tilt the foot up, the top part of the shoe clips/cuts through the leg. You could keep working on the leg, but eventually, you would find that the shoe forces some unrealistic cavities in the leg. In this case, we can give the foot a little bit of flex. Simply select the shin bone and add the smallest amount of weight to the tongue of the shoe.

If all is done well, you might end up with something like this:

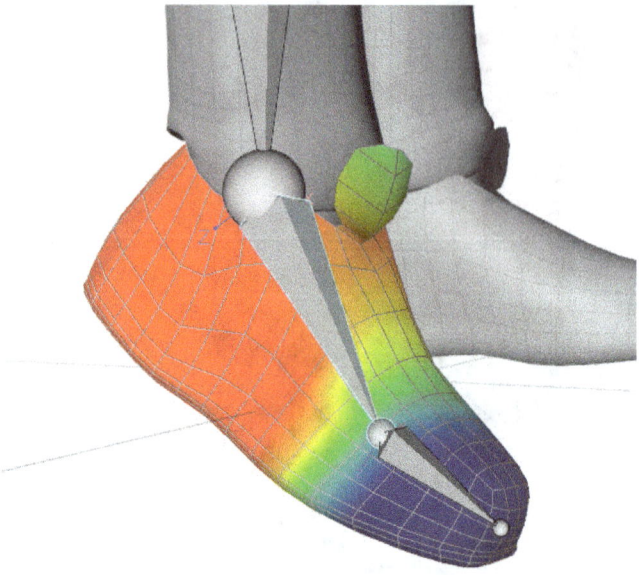

Figure 5.15 – The shoe mesh weights adjusted

Note how the tongue of the shoe (that's the flat flap at the front of the ankle) requires just the slightest amount of weight to conform to the rest of the leg. Adjusting weights while in stress poses is critical to getting your desired result. Bend, paint, bend, paint, bend, paint, and so on.

While the feet might seem a small part, it covers a large part of the skill needed to weight-paint, as it involves active problem-solving and attention to detail. Finish the rest of the foot, and you will be ready to move on to the knees and the rest.

Rigging the knee

Let's move on to the knee, which is exceptionally simple. There are two things to note here – **creases** and **curves**.

Think about your knee – if you bend it, the *front of the knee produces a nice curve* while the *inside of your knee becomes folded*. We can replicate this with weights. A tight gradient will produce a crease while a large smooth gradient will produce a curve.

The following diagrams show some ideal weights for you to aim for – sharp in the crease and soft in the bend:

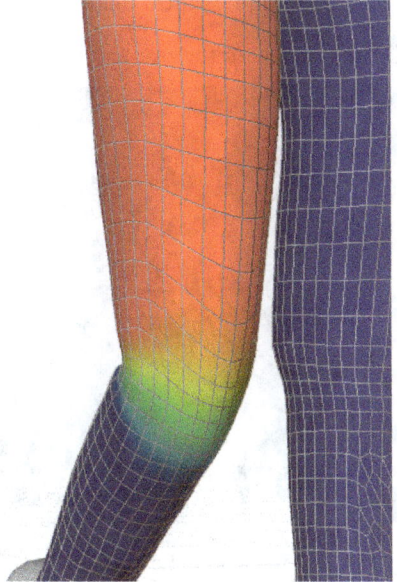

Figure 5.16 – The front of the knee weights

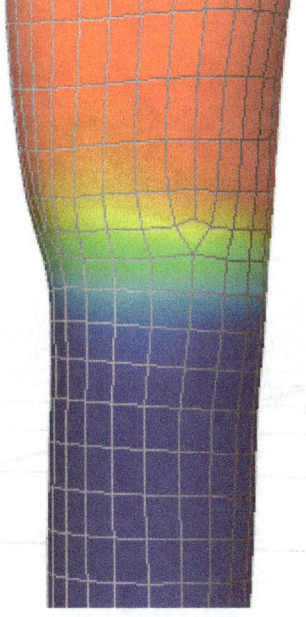

Figure 5.17 – The rear of the knee weights

Remember to place the bones in stress poses, and then bring the leg up to see how it looks. If the leg creases and folds too much, smooth the weights out. If there's not enough folding and the back of the leg does not close properly, make your handoff gradient tighter.

The following diagram shows the final result for the rear part of our knee:

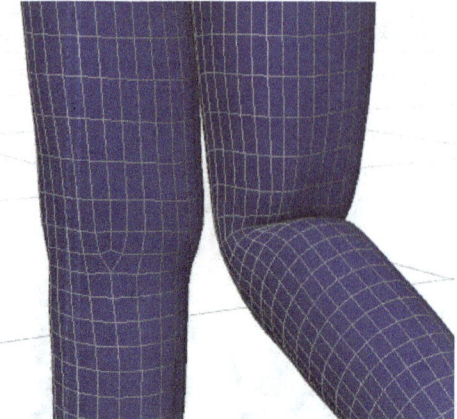

Figure 5.18 – The rear of the knee final result

With the feet and lower legs done, we're nearly finished with the lower half of the body. We will finish it by completing the hips in the following section.

Rigging the hips

Moving onto the hip region, I'll give you a general idea of what I normally do to rig the hips:

1. Selecting the thigh bone, paint the whole of the upper leg.

    Figure 5.19 shows some very rough weights, which is how my weights start out before I go ahead and refine them.

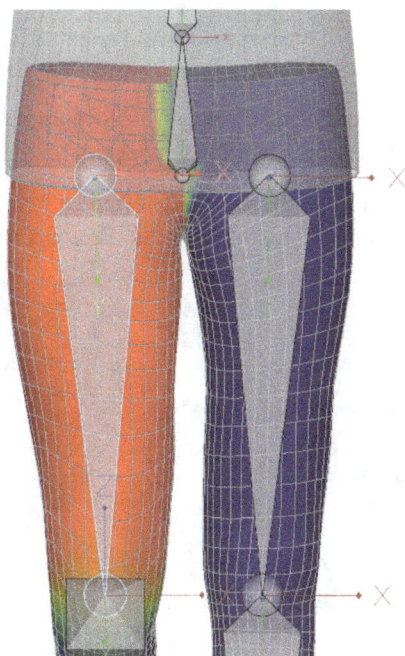

Figure 5.19 – The thigh weights started

2. Selecting the base of the spine, paint a rough belt where you expect the legs to bend. It doesn't need to be too precise for now; use the smoothing tool to smooth any rough work later. *Figure 5.19* shows my rough work for the hips:

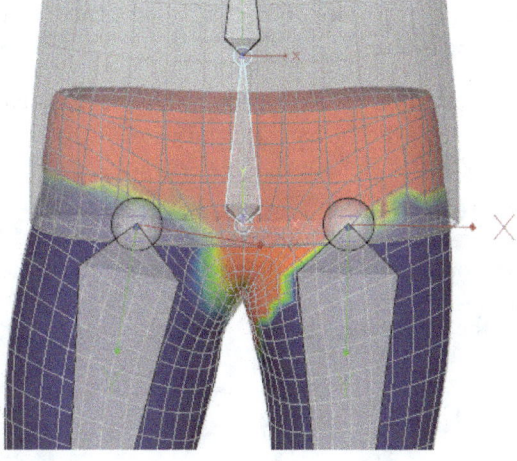

Figure 5.20 – The rough groin area weights

3. Then, smooth out all the weights between the leg and spine to clean things up and get a better idea of what's going on.

4. Push the leg into some stress positions, and when you encounter any positions that do not look right, hold the leg there and edit your weights to your desired result.

In my work, I found that the front of the leg was deformed too much. By going into **Edit Mode** on the armature, I could push the bone closer to the affected area and reduce the distortion.

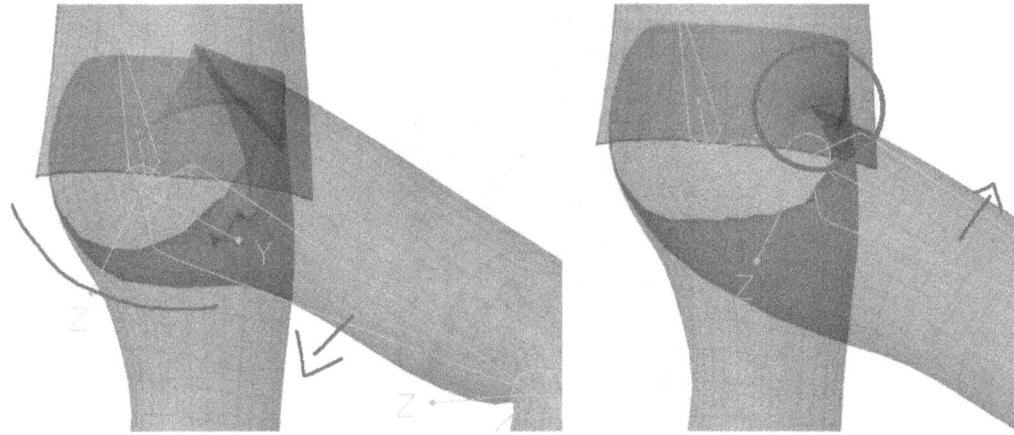

Figure 5.21 – Bone placement and deformation

In the preceding diagram, you can see how *pushing the bone toward the back* gives *better results for the back*, while *pushing it forward* gives *better results for the front*. What you go for depends on your use case.

I pushed the thigh bone forward by just 1/4th of the thigh to give more focus and definition to the front, while not completely losing the back.

Feel free to spend time on any part to get it looking nice; it's not too important, as we can come back to make touchups, but you could hide the top half here and get the leg creases up to a good standard.

Fixing clipping on the hips

For the second half of this section, we need to fix the coat clipping into the leg:

1. We'll start by painting the lower torso like so:

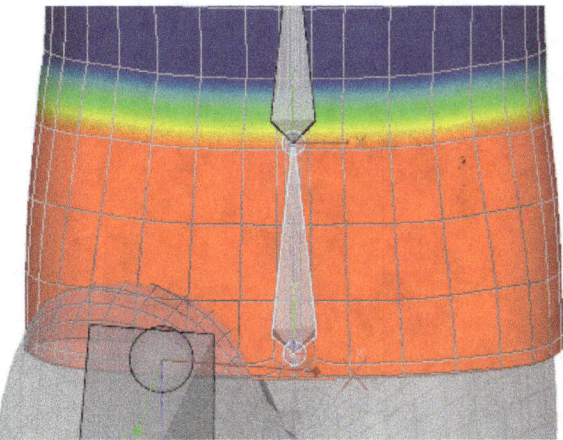

Figure 5.22 – The initial lower torso weights

2. We will select the leg and paint the top. Giving the leg authority over the coat will allow it to push the coat up and out of the way.

3. So, selecting the leg as posed, push it up, start painting the shirt around the leg, and note how it begins to conform to the thigh bone, with the intersecting becoming less of a problem. Get this to a reasonable quality, and then carry on with the rest of the spine.

Note how we blanket-painted the lower torso and then painted the leg, with Blender automatically subtracting the leg weights from the torso bone. This is so that you don't end up jumping between meshes, endlessly trying to balance out the weights. Essentially, painting over an area that already has weights will remove the old weights and replace them with new ones, belonging to whichever bone you have selected.

The following diagram shows the final result of my work. Maybe there's room for improvement, but as it stands, it will do just fine.

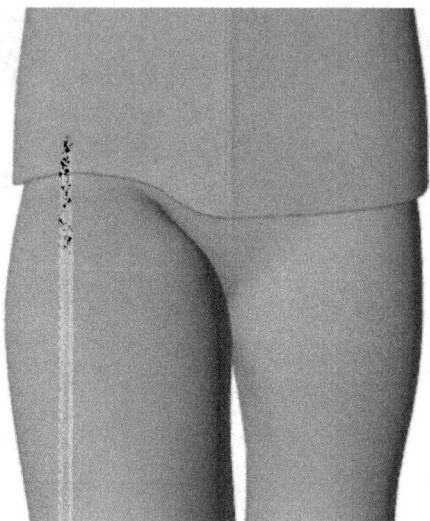

Figure 5.23 – The leg and torso final result

Figure 5.23 shows how I have left the legs/torso, but there's definitely room for improvement. Where you draw the line for quality is completely up to you.

With the lower half of the body done, you have learned all the core skills needed to carry on further up. However, I'll still give some guidance as we move on to the spine. The spine is super simple; the shoulders, however, are much more laborious, as we will find out later.

Rigging the spine

Rigging the spine is a relatively easy and quick affair. We'll only encounter problems as we approach the upper chest/shoulders.

Paint a generalized area for the second bone in the spine. We already have some weight for the first bone from doing the legs. *Figure 5.24* shows a rough weighted region for the second bone in the spine chain. There's a good chance you already know what region you want to paint for this bone; however, things do become more complex further up the spine.

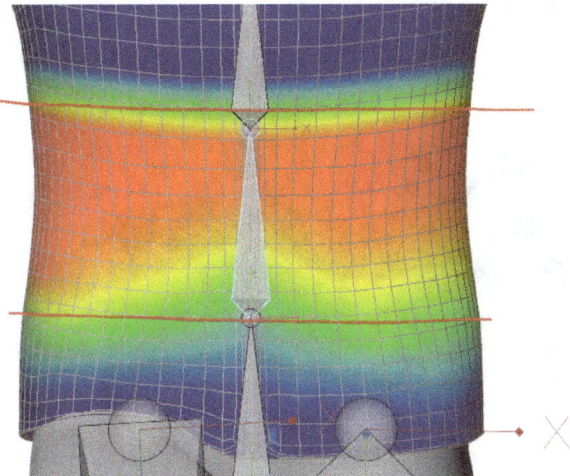

Figure 5.24 – The spine weight regions

Aim for your handoffs to land close to these lines, as this follows the joints of the spine. Once you have painted some rough weights, put the second bone in the spine into stress positions – forward, back, and side to side.

The side-to-side position might show clipping from the pants; that's because the second bone shifts the geometry too far down, so you should reduce its reach and shift its weights higher up. Alternatively, if you are confident that the spine is right and the hips are wrong, you can do the reverse and have the hips follow the bones further up the spine just enough to hide the clipping. *Figure 5.25* shows how avoiding clipping on the waist can have a knock-on effect further up the body.

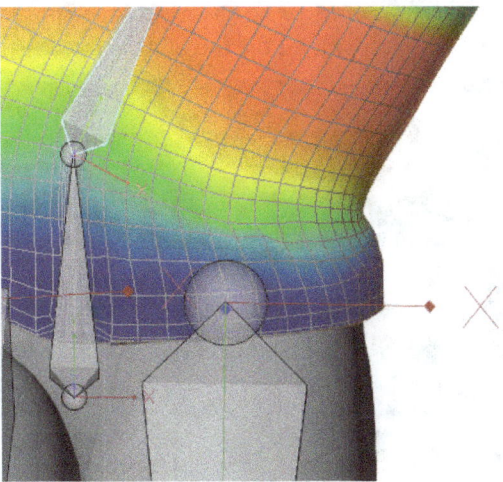

Figure 5.25 – A harsh gradient on the spine-to-hips handoff

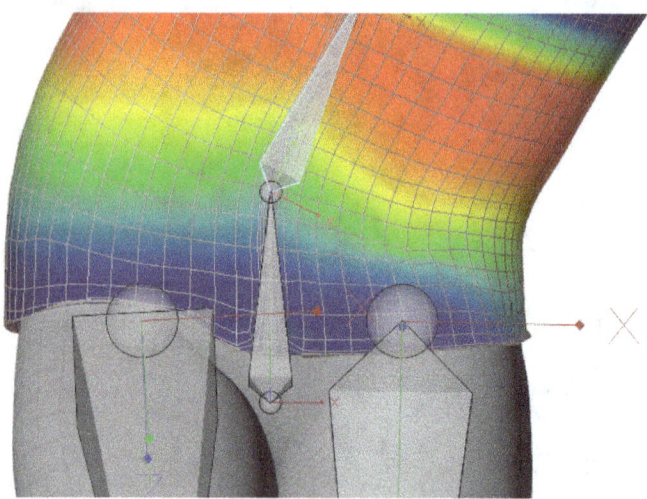

Figure 5.26 – A smooth spine-to-hips handoff

Between *Figure 5.25* and *Figure 5.26*, you can see how smoothing out that gradient gave a more natural curve at the sides of the torso.

Remember that a stress position should still be humanly possible; tying the rig into a wild knot proves nothing and gives a false reading for real-world usage. Only go as far as you think an animator would, which is likely to be average flexibility.

This is no quick task; you're going to need to jump from bone to bone to bone, trying many different combinations. Every model and rig is different, but with experience, you will be able to identify zones of weight control before you even start.

The following diagram shows you my first pass for the rest of the torso/chest area.

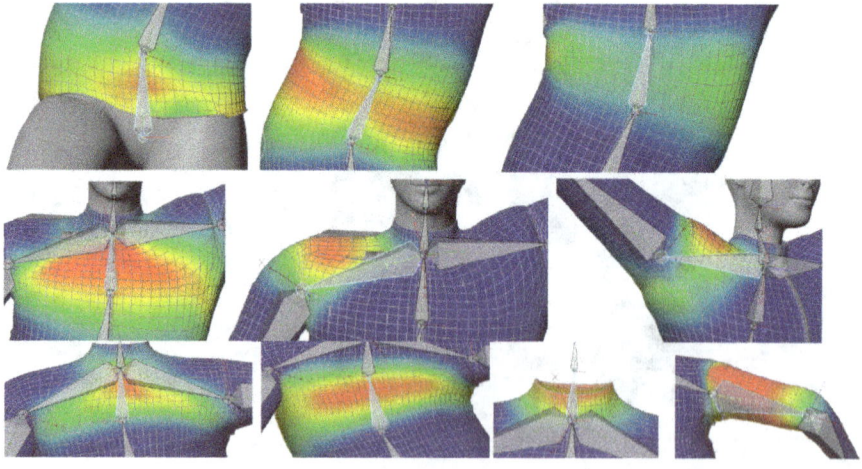

Figure 5.27 – My first pass at the weights

We use the term *passes* to signify revisions of work, usually based on given feedback. The first pass may be rough, sometimes missing certain things. Depending on what's needed, you will most likely have to come back and make a whole host of changes and fixes to your work. Nothing is final; there's always room for improvement for everyone. Getting a working product is the most important thing; you can refine it further down the line.

Using *Figure 5.27*, go ahead and paint the rest of the chest area and upper arms. Here are some handy pointers:

- Both the shoulder and arm control the armpit, and some chest weight can be added as needed.

- Stress poses are the only way you will work out where your weights need to be.

- Sometimes, the answer lies elsewhere. We can get so caught up on a particular bone when it might be another bone elsewhere that's secretly exerting influence. If you come across a situation like this, then go and give all the other bones a wiggle and check that they're not controlling the wrong areas. The **Auto Normalize** option has a habit of causing this.

With most of the body done, we'll now move on to the hands. Hands are difficult not in their complexity but due to how fingers occlude each other, making it very difficult to paint exactly what you were intending to paint.

You will need very fine camera control, so here is a reminder of the controls for the camera.

Quick shortcuts

Focus – . (on the numpad), **Zoom** – *scroll wheel*, **Pan** – *MMB (middle mouse button)*, **Lateral**– *MMB + Shift*, and **Orthographic sides** – *Alt + MMB*

Rigging the hands

Hands are one of the most awkward parts of weight painting in Blender. Very small geometry packed together tightly means painting the correct parts can be a hassle, but the basic concept is just the same as the rest of the body. Take a guess, paint it, stress it, and fix it.

The following diagrams show some ideal starting weights; feel free to use these as a guide:

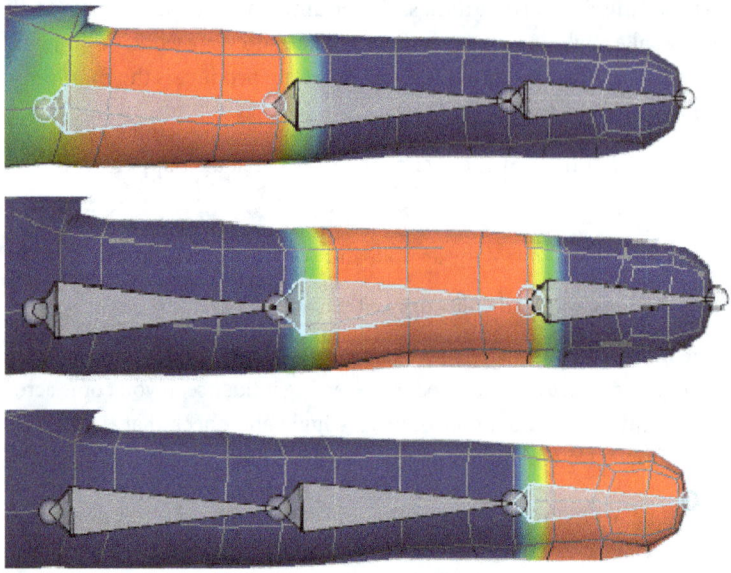

Figure 5.28 – Finger segment weights

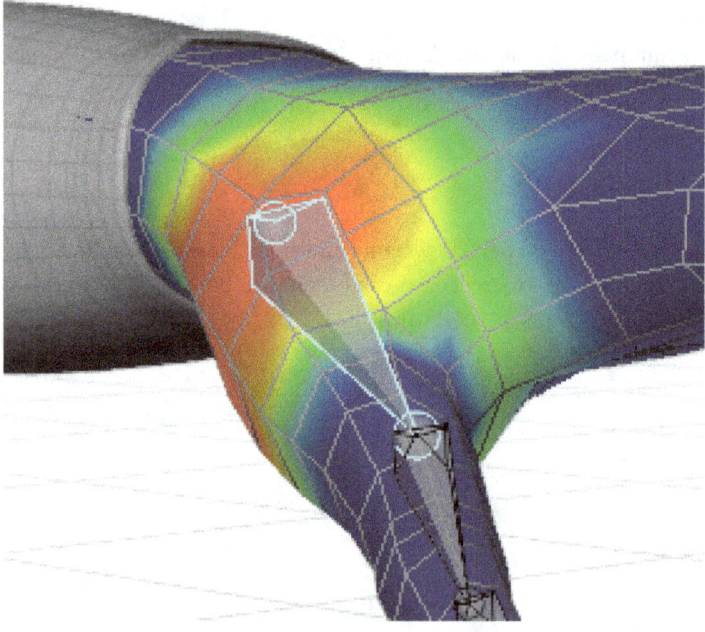

Figure 5.29 – Thumb base weights

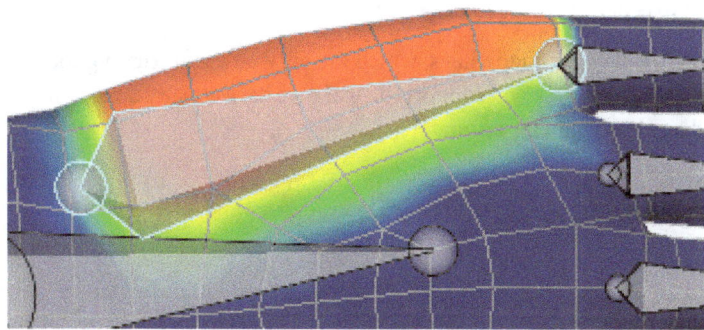

Figure 5.30 – The metacarpal bone (used for squeezing motions)

Oftentimes, you may intend to paint one finger but end up hitting other fingers. It's easy to miss sometimes, but when stressing the fingers, observe each one to see whether any geometry moves unintentionally.

For areas that are hard to reach, you can often use the Blur tool. If surrounding weights are at 1.0 the result of the Blur tool will be close enough to 1.0, in-between fingers is a prime place to use the Blur tool.

If you find that the inside of the fingers creases too much, pull the bones down toward the inside, and if the outside distorts too much, push the bones up.

Once you think you are finished, move the fingers around. If some fingers pull the skin of their neighboring fingers, feel free to move and bend the fingers out of the way. I like to paint the index finger first and then bend it 180 degrees into the hand to hide it, clearing my view of the next finger.

Summary

We started this chapter by parenting a mesh to an armature with empty weight groups, giving us a clean slate to work with. We then moved on to weight paint mode, using the draw tool to set weights and the Blur tool to soften the border between different weight zones. We continued by covering the rest of the body, front and back, with the figure diagrams serving as guidance. Finally, we applied some touchups while bending the rig into stress positions to find poor deformation.

- Used *Ctrl + P* to parent a mesh to an armature, selecting the mesh and then the armature

- Selected an empty weights option to give us a clean start

- Experimented with how bone placement can affect deformation quality

- Followed the provided diagrams for rough guidance on the zones each bone should control

That concludes this chapter – you now know how to take any mesh and any armature and bind them together to bring models to life.

In the next chapter, we will cover **shape keys**, which are very powerful rigging tools that allow us to deform a mesh without bones. They will support the work we have already done with more fine tuning and quality, applied automatically for animators.

Part 3: Advanced Techniques

In this final part, more advanced techniques and additions will be covered, including the **Inverse Kinematics (IK)** constraint, shape keys, and handy edge-case tricks to produce more advanced rigs.

This part has the following chapters:

- *Chapter 6, Using IK and Rig Controls*
- *Chapter 7, Getting Started with Shape Keys*
- *Chapter 8, Beyond the Basics*

Using IK and Rig Controls

Inverse Kinematics (IK) is a tool we can use to automatically pose bones based on a few inputs. IK is typically composed of two handles, a target and a pole. The target is the point in space where the IK system tries to get the end bone to match and the pole controls the direction of deflection. Its primary use is for rapid and precise animation but it can be used beyond animation in some edge cases.

By the end of this chapter, you will understand the differences between IK and FK and when to use each one. You will have a rig featuring an IK setup for both the legs and the arms that allows animators to work with tools they are most comfortable with, saving time and energy on their part.

In this chapter, we will cover the following topics:

- Understanding IK and FK

- Understanding the effects of IK and FK in animation

- Preparation for IK

- Adding the IK constraint

- Applying IK to the legs

- Constraints on handles

Understanding IK and FK

Before we move on to creating our own IK system, we should get a grasp of what IK and FK are. If you have experience in animation then you likely already know this. If you do not know the difference or need a refresher, the following subsections offer detailed explanations of both IK and FK.

Forward Kinematics

Rotating every bone one at a time into a pose is known as **Forward Kinematics (FK)**.

In an FK chain, each successive bone inherits the rotation of the previous bone and is not affected by bones further up the chain. While it may feel like a very rigid system, it's surprisingly the most effective way for animators to produce large sweeping arcs and precise movements. Its downside is that it requires an immense amount of effort and time to work with, so much so that it's the much less frequently used of the two modes.

You may recognize this pose method because it's what you have been using throughout the book to pose any of your bones.

Inverse Kinematics

A chain of bones that automatically work together to target a specific, dynamic point in space is known as **Inverse Kinematics (IK)**.

In an IK chain, each bone progressively works towards a set point in space. When this point is moved, the chain will update to follow. This makes the control of each bone in the chain automatic. A crucial part of IK is how it manages to fit the whole chain in between the starting point and the targeted point. If the point is further away than the length of the chain, you will get the result of a perfectly straight chain. However, if the target is shorter than the chain then the IK solver will seem to *bend* the chain to fit it into the distance between the start and target. The direction of bending is defined by the **pole** target (more on that later).

Now that you understand what IK and FK are and how they work, we can move on to the effects they have in animation and why we have IK and FK in the first place.

Understanding the effects of IK and FK in animation

While you may not be an aspiring animator, it's somewhat important that you understand some key theories within animation. This knowledge will allow you to decide where to use FK and IK on rigs. If you can preemptively decide what system belongs where, you can save a lot of time and people will appreciate your work just that little bit more. In general, IK goes on arms and legs while FK fills in the gaps such as the spine, neck, fingers, and toes.

In the real world nothing organic moves in straight lines; all of our motions occur in arcs. From humans walking to birds flying, there is never a straight line. In animation, straight lines are a result of linear interpolation between two points. Take a look at *Figure 6.1* and *Figure 6.2*, which show how FK and IK systems move from keyframe to keyframe when animating.

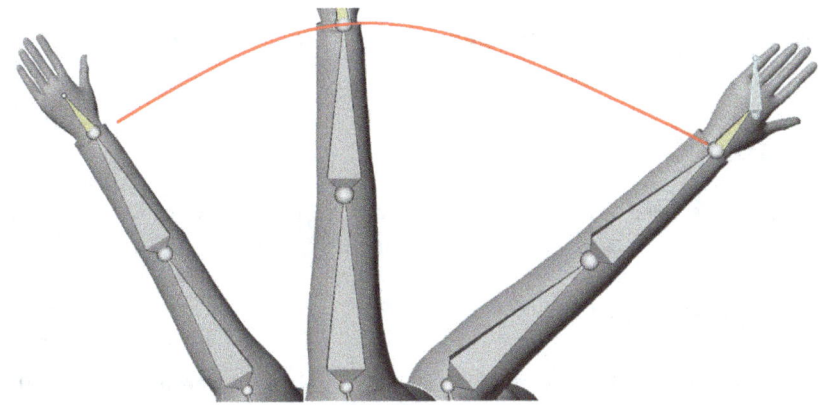

Figure 6.1 – FK controls form a clear arc

Inverse kinematics form a linear line because the interpolation is position based, and not rotation based as is the case with FK.

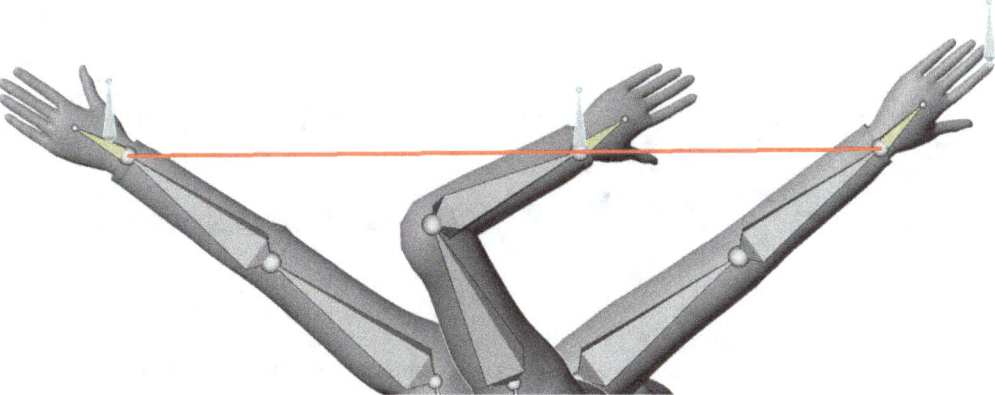

Figure 6.2 – IK controls produce a linear line

IK is best used for the precise control of limbs – a hand here and a foot there, with no margin for error. Hands and feet are a primary example, as we can't have feet sliding and hands missing their targets or sliding around. IK can also be exponentially faster than FK. Using one control for multiple bones is bound to save time.

Other parts of a character will be better suited to FK, such as a long, winding tail. Tails move in arcs and usually lack the level of precision seen with other limbs.

The arms and legs on our rig are best suited to IK. The speed and ease of use that IK delivers are perfect for a generic humanoid character, so we will use IK for the arms and legs in this chapter, but you're free to experiment with both systems.

With this explanation of why you might choose one system over the other, we can move on to a basic IK setup.

Preparing for IK

There are some things we need to do before we add the IK constraint. We need to adjust the bones that will be in the chain and add some new bones for the IK system.

Pre-bending IK chains

The IK constraint isn't very smart – take a look at *Figure 6.2* and notice how the elbow bends the way we expect it to. Chances are that the IK constraint will choose to bend the elbow the wrong way just because it has no concept of a human elbow.

Thankfully, there's a way for us to show it how to bend and it is pretty simple. We take the arm bones into Edit Mode and give it a slight bend at the elbow. This preexisting bend tells the IK what direction it should bend in when animating a movement.

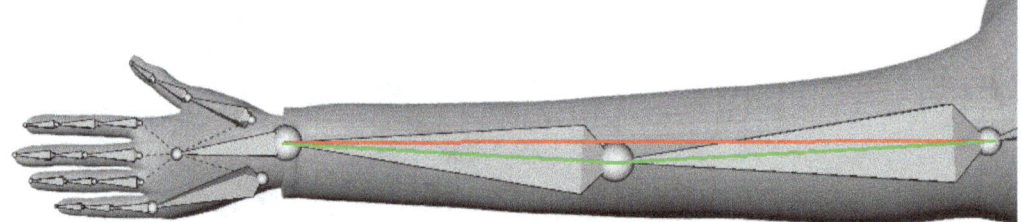

Figure 6.3 – Elbow bend

Shown in *Figure 6.3* is the little bend I gave the bones by grabbing the elbow joint in **Edit Mode** and just sliding it toward the back of the arm a little.

Adding control bones

We're going to make two bones. If you take a look at *Figure 1.1* (The collection of images at the start of the book) in *Chapter 1*, you will see the floating bones used for controlling the rig. Some appear as extra, colorful objects and others are just normal disconnected bones. We're making those very extra bones now. In the example I provide, I work on the left-hand side of the model. When we get to the IK constraint itself, I will explain what each of these bones is for.

To make the new bones for the IK system, follow these steps:

1. Enter **Edit Mode** while keeping the armature selected.

2. Select the hand bone we are adding IK to and duplicate the bone, raising this duplicated bone above the hand to differentiate between them, and renaming this bone `Hand.L.IK` or `Hand.R.IK` depending on which side you have chosen. This is the **Target bone.**

3. We are also going to make the **Pole bone**. We'll see more details on this when the IK constraint is completed and working. For now, just duplicate the Hand IK bone and **move it behind the elbow**. You can name this bone `Pole.L.IK` or `Pole.R.IK` respectively.

> **Important note**
>
> **Duplicating bones will also duplicate any constraints they have**, so these new bones will have the IK constraint we applied before. You will know these bones have this IK constraint if they have a unique color. You must delete any IK constraints on these new bones, as only the hand should have IK. They will also still be parented to the arm, which will cause a dependency loop, so make sure you **clear the parent** with *Alt + P*. If there is a dotted line between any of these new bones then you must clear the parent. (In short – *Alt + P* these 2 new bones).

Once done, you should have two new bones as shown in *Figure 6.4*:

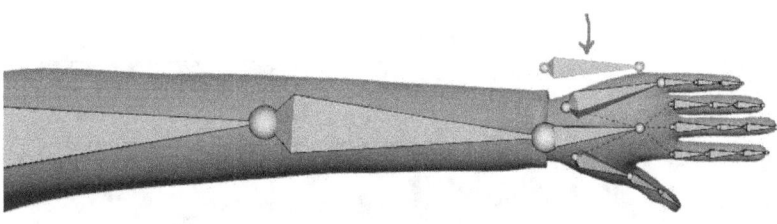

Figure 6.4 – IK bones added

With all the necessary bones named and in place, we can move on to the IK constraint, where all the magic happens.

Adding the IK constraint

In this first IK setup, we will cover the configuration of a very basic single IK constraint on the hands. A **constraint** is just a function in Blender that limits/modifies how an element might behave. In our case, we will be working with **bone constraints**.

Head into Pose Mode with our armature selected, select either of the hands and head on over to the **Bone constraints** tab, pictured in *Figure 6.5*. Then, add an **Inverse Kinematics** bone constraint.

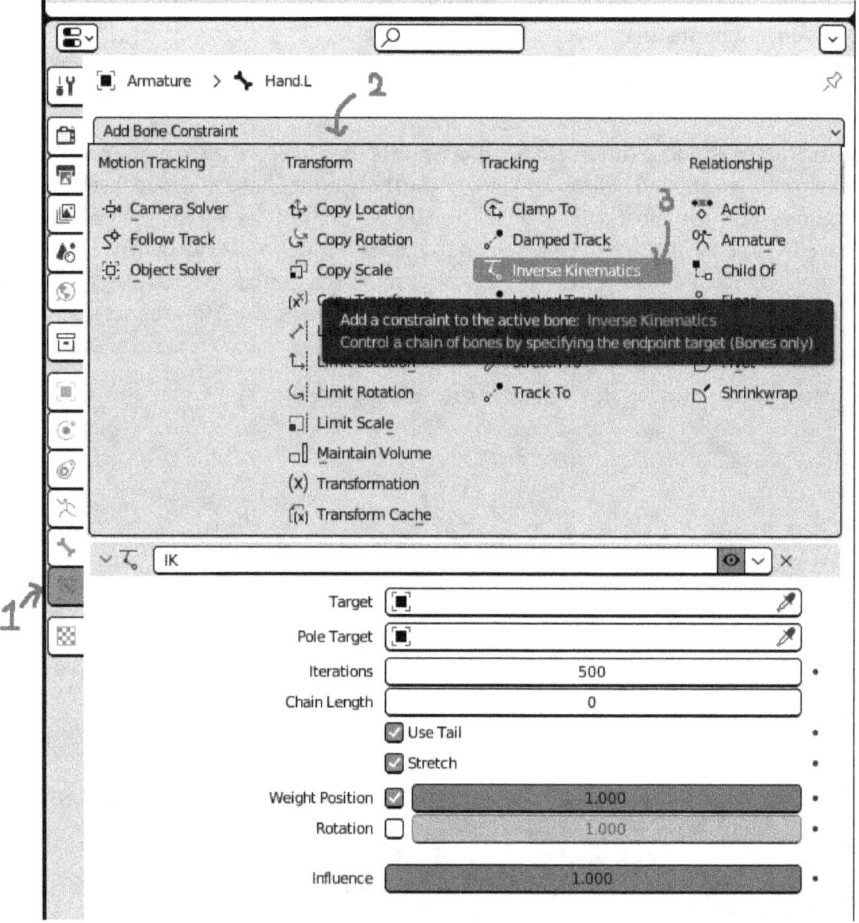

Figure 6.5 – IK constraint added

The steps to add the constraint are shown in *Figure 6.5*, but the navigation should be somewhat familiar by now. With this IK constraint added you will see plenty of boxes for us to fill. We will cover each box in descending order, starting with the **Target** field.

Target:

1. Click the box next to **Target** and select the armature. There should only be one armature in the scene.

2. A new box appears directly below asking for a bone. Click this and set it to the target bone made just before, which should be named **Hand.L.IK**.

Pole:

1. Click the box next to **Pole Target** and select the armature. There should only be one armature in the scene.

2. A new box has appeared directly below asking for a bone. Click this and set it to the pole bone made just before, which should be named **Pole.L.IK**.

After completing the preceding instructions, you will notice the rig move as it adjusts to the new target we have set. However, we still haven't given the IK constraint all the information it needs so at the moment the results you are seeing are not what we intend. Let's finish this constraint and get the IK system up and running.

There are a few more things left for us to do, starting with the important *Pole angle* and *Chain length*.

Chain length

Before adjusting this, untick **Use Tail** (more on this later in the *Use Tail* section).

Chain length is simply how many bones we are going to be controlling with this constraint. It is currently set to 1, meaning we are only controlling the hand bone, but we want our IK system to control the whole arm. Set the chain length to 2, which will allow the control to extend up to the upper arm, leaving the shoulder out. If you go ahead and grab the target bone and move it, you will see the rest of the arm move with it. If you had a chain length of 10, the next 10 bones in the chain would all be under the control of the IK constraint.

Pole angle

The pole target simply controls what direction the IK chain bends in. In our example, this will allow us to move the elbow up and down. The angle controls this relation and the angle used changes depending on how the rig is made.

The only way to find this angle is by trial and error. Start by pushing the hand in towards the body and pulling the pole bone away from the arm. Then click and drag the box, using it as a slider to find the angle that aligns the elbow with the pole bone. Both the setup used and the result after finding my angle are shown in *Figure 6.6*. I came to a figure of 150 degrees, but your angle may vary, so be sure to find the precise angle that produces the results you want.

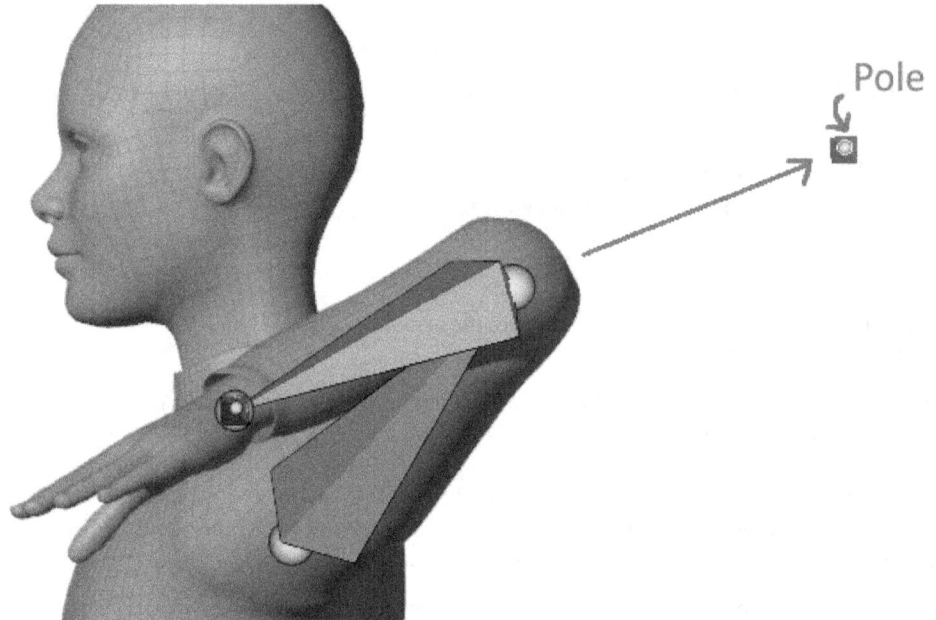

Figure 6.6 - Pole angle

Figure 6.6 shows how a pole angle of 150 degrees makes the elbow perfectly align with the pole control.

Use Tail

This simply sets the target of the IK constraint to either the head or the tail of the target bone. Untick **Use Tail** for now so that the hand bone sits inside the target bone. This also affects the chain length, as when ticked it will incorporate the hand bone into the IK chain.

Weight Position, Rotation, and Influence

These options simply control the influence of the IK constraint. Unless you are trying to make a complex system to achieve a specific goal, you shouldn't need to change these. **Rotation** is the exception; this allows you to control the hand bone rotation with the target bone. When you make the rig look fancy by adding custom handles and hiding bones, this becomes useful. It lets us hide the hand bone and just use the target bone to control the arm and hand.

> **Important note**
>
> **Stretch** and **Iterations** can be ignored for now. If you want to find out more about them, head on over to the Blender documentation at `https://docs.blender.org/manual/en/latest/`. With all of the preceding tasks done, you now have your first IK setup! It's basic, sure, as well as a little bland and stale looking, but that will be addressed. Feel free to play around with the target and pole bones to see how they behave. When you want to reset everything, you can select all the bones, bring up the search bar with *F3*, and type `Clear transform` to bring up the **Pose | Clear Transforms | All** options to reset the pose.

Applying IK to the legs

The idea behind the legs is identical to the arms. I'll give a recap and show you what it should look like.

The quick steps are as follows:

1. Add an IK constraint to the foot bone.

2. Make two new bones, `Foot.L.IK` and `Leg.L.Pole`, and clear the parents with *Alt + P*.

3. Place the IK bone in front of the ankle and the pole in front of the knee.

4. Bend the knee in Edit Mode just as you did for the arm.

5. Set the target and pole to the respective bones.

6. Untick **Stretch** and set the chain length.

7. Push the target bone up to bend the leg, move the pole to the side, and adjust the pole angle so that the knee points towards the pole bone.

With all that done, you should have something similar to the following:

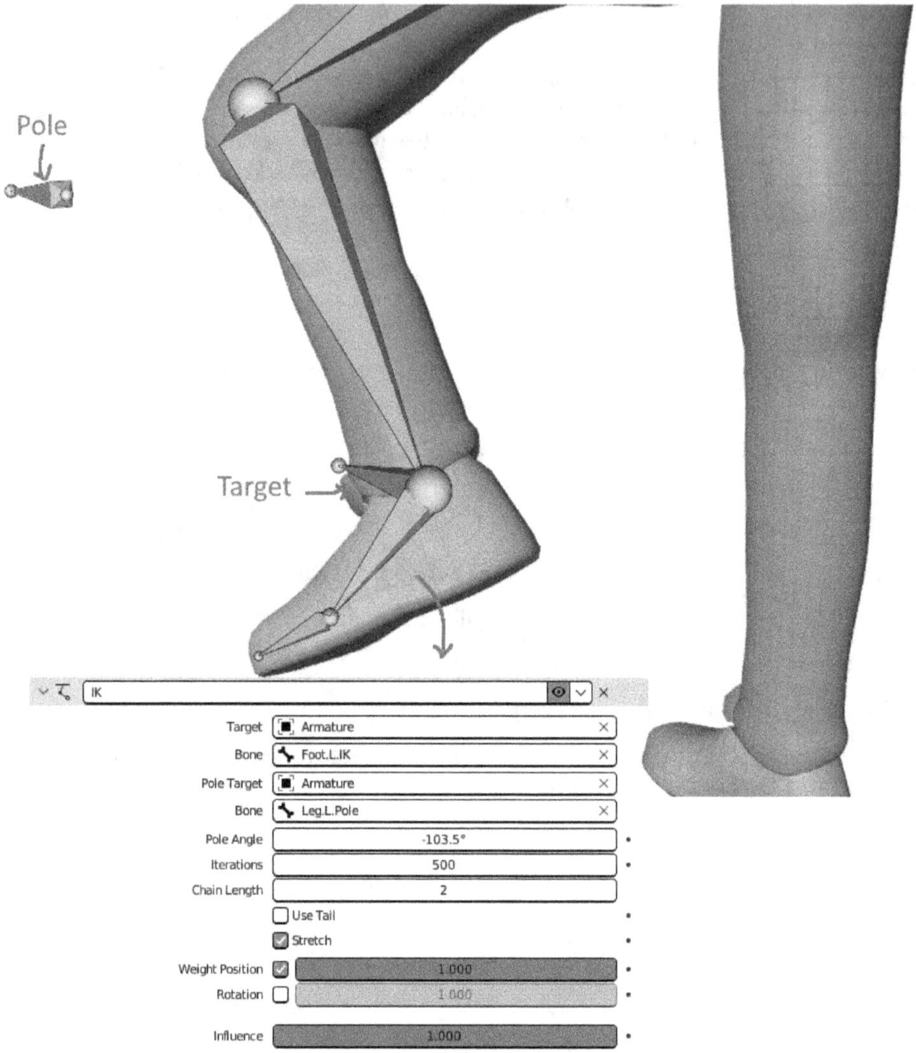

Figure 6.7 – IK setup with bones and constraints

Figure 6.7 shows the whole setup for the legs. Some of your values may be different so if you don't get the correct result at first, just have a play around with the constraint.

Constraints on handles

A more advanced trick you can use is to place constraints on handles to change how they are used and prevent the rig from going places it's not meant to.

A simple example is the **Limit Location** constraint, which can be used as an artificial floor for the wheels of a vehicle, as follows:

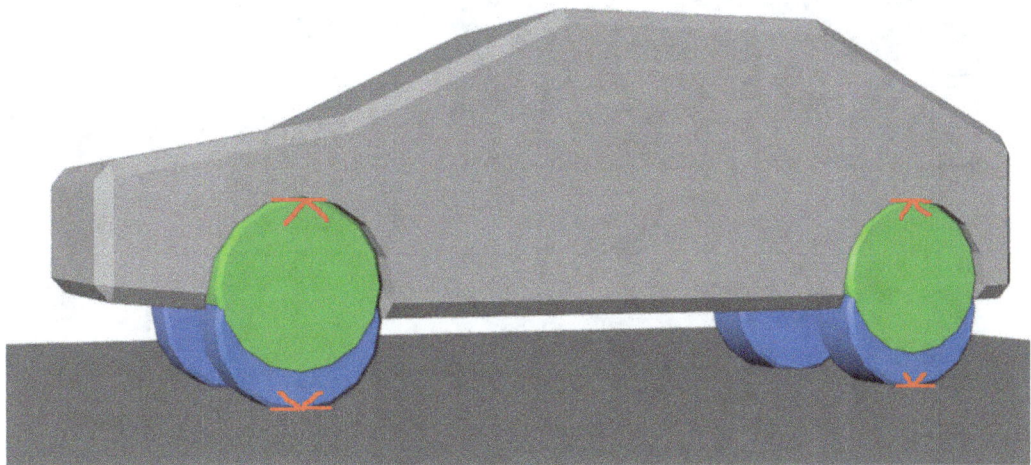

Figure 6.8 – Car with constraints

The pictured vehicle has many constraints to keep the wheel above the ground and keep the body above the wheel. No matter how much you push the car down, its wheel will not go through the floor and the body will not go through the wheel.

Take a look at the **Add Bone Constraint** dropdown to see the range of constraints available. Their names explain what they do for the most part.

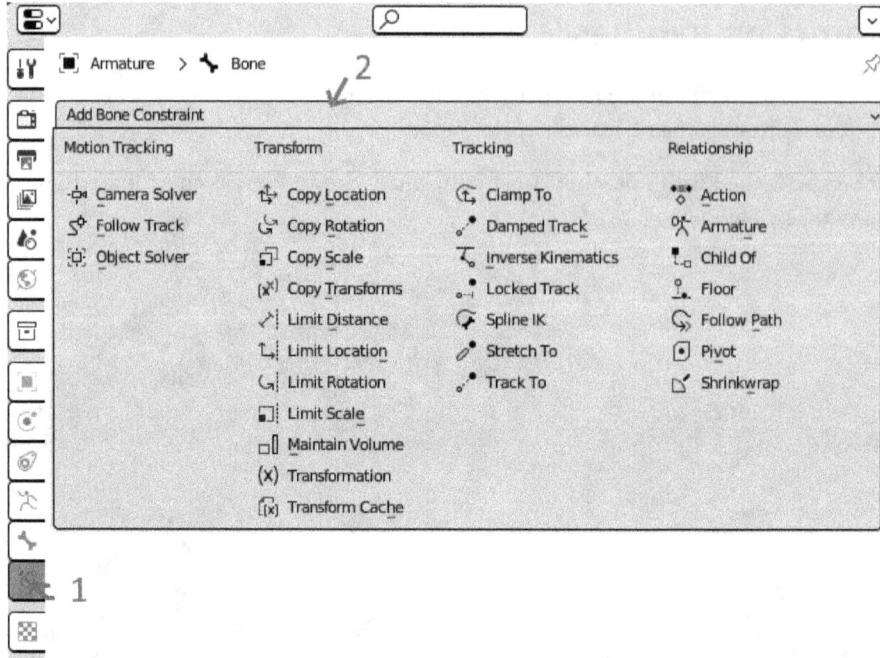

Figure 6.9 – The Add Bone Constraint dropdown

If you are ever unsure of a particular feature, just check the Blender documentation; failing that, there are always quick videos online showing how to use a certain feature in detail.

Constraints on bones are usually made at the request of animators. There's an infinite arrangement of constraints that you may need to mix to get your desired result. Stacking constraints is a little out of scope but feel free to try and get a few working and see what happens.

Summary

In this chapter, we covered the uses of IK and FK and how they worked. We moved on to the IK constraint and learned about the function and purpose of each part of the constraint, starting with adding the supporting pole and target bones to adjusting the chain length and pole angle.

With the knowledge from this chapter and the previous ones under your belt, you should be able to approach many rigging tasks with a solid understanding, from adding bones to weight painting and now using constraints to modify how the rig is controlled.

While the rig is currently functional, there are still many small features you can add to make this rig a brilliant piece of work!

The next chapter will cover shape keys and drivers, using bones to apply hand-sculpted effects to the mesh in ways that simple weight painting cannot achieve.

7

Getting Started with Shape Keys

In this chapter, we will cover shape keys, going from a basic introduction to getting hands-on with making and modifying our own shape keys. After covering shape keys, we will discover how bone drivers can be used to automate the input for these shape keys, activating them based on bone movement.

In this chapter, we will cover the following topics:

- Introducing shape keys
- Making a shape key
- Editing a shape key
- Using drivers
- Mirroring shape keys

By the end of this chapter, you will be able to add, remove, and modify shape keys to fix poor deformations and will know how to make shape keys an automatic part of a rig.

Introducing shape keys

Shape keys are an exceptionally powerful and infinitely versatile system that stores the local position of every vertex. Shape keys are essentially a stored shape that a mesh can take using the current set of vertices.

A shape key consists of two elements, a base and the shape we want to morph into. Shape keys are relative to the base shape, meaning that instead of holding a specific shape, they hold a delta (i.e., the difference) from the base to the target shape.

This idea of shape keys being deltas might sound strange at first, but it's this very trait that gives them their power. It means we can start from a base shape, add a shape key, then add another one on top, or even subtract shape keys. This means any part of the mesh can be modified by multiple shape keys, with each shape key adding or subtracting its own shape to produce an almost procedural result.

How can we use them? In the form of **corrective shape keys**. Corrective shape keys allow us to fix simple deformation issues without resorting to using a greater number of bones than any animator can be expected to work with. These corrective shape keys can be the solution to poor deformation with complex geometry. If weight painting can't fix your problem, shape keys can. In the following section, we set up the premise of this chapter, fixing poor deformation in the glutes of a character. This area is a typical shape key target and will be great for learning the basics.

Example of poor deformation

Take a look at *Figure 7.1* and see how the glute muscle of our model doesn't deform correctly. It's nowhere near what we want. While we can mitigate this with very careful weights and mindful geometry, doing so would be a waste of time and produce inferior results in comparison to what we're going to do with shape keys (oh, and **drivers** – more on that in the later *Using drivers* section).

The following figure shows an example of poor deformation. This area of the model will be the focus of this chapter:

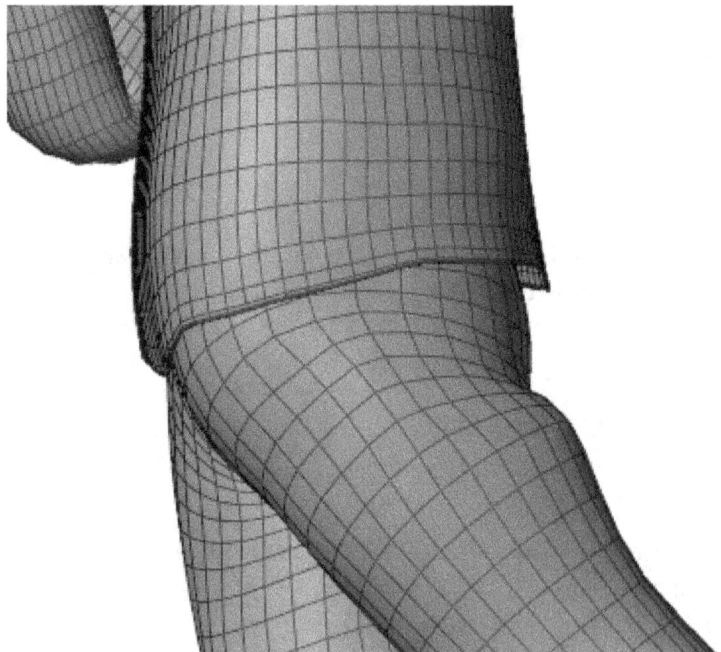

Figure 7.1 – Poor deformation – No shape keys

First, we need to add the shape keys. Starting with the base key, it's important we have a base key because that's what stores our default mesh and allows us to transition from that default to the modified shape keys. It's not all too uncommon for people to forget the base key and end up wasting a massive amount of time on useless shape keys that have no basis to function from.

Making a shape key

This section will start us off by getting to grips with adding shape keys, covering the menus that you will need to navigate to create these shape keys. Working on the basis and then creating the additional shape keys that we can edit later on:

1. Let's look at how to make a shape key. The first one will automatically be named **Basis**, our base shape key. To add a new shape key, navigate to **Object data properties | Shape keys** and click the + button.

    This new shape key will automatically be named **Basis**. Do not delete or modify this in any way. **Basis** stores the base mesh without modifications and is what any subsequent shape keys spring from. This navigation process is shown in order in *Figure 7.2*:

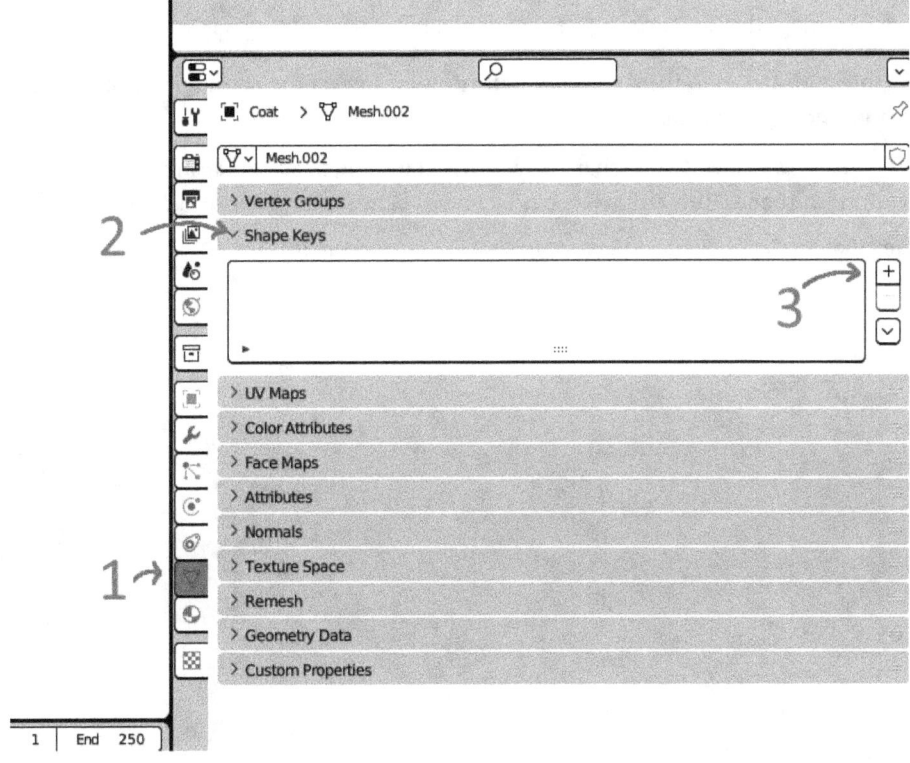

Figure 7.2 – Navigating to the Shape Keys UI

2. Now that you have a base shape key, go ahead and click the + button again to add our first real shape key.

3. You should give each shape key a name that makes it easy to decipher its purpose. You can do this by double-clicking the name in question. For example, I named my shape key `Upper_Leg.L_Corective_Backwards` because the upper leg bone is what we plan on using to drive this key automatically and what the shape key will correct when the leg swings backward.

So now you have a base shape key and another shape key that we will edit to fix the deformation of the glute. With this in place, let's move to Edit Mode to make this corrective shape key.

Editing a shape key

In this section, we're going to take the shape key we made previously and modify it, as the shape key as it stands currently is not much use. This section will be making heavy use of **Edit Mode** and **Proportional Editing**.

In Edit Mode, we will modify this shape key manually to fix the poor deformation using the same controls covered in *Chapter 2* to select vertices and move them into position.

There are a few things that we need to take care of before we start editing our shape key:

1. In **Object Mode**, go to the **Armature deform modifier** on the mesh and select **Edit Mode: Display modifier in Edit mode**.

    This means as you edit your shape key, you will be able to see the result when the mesh is following the bones. This removes the need to flick between modes in a trial-and-error fashion.

    The following screenshot shows how to show your work in Edit Mode:

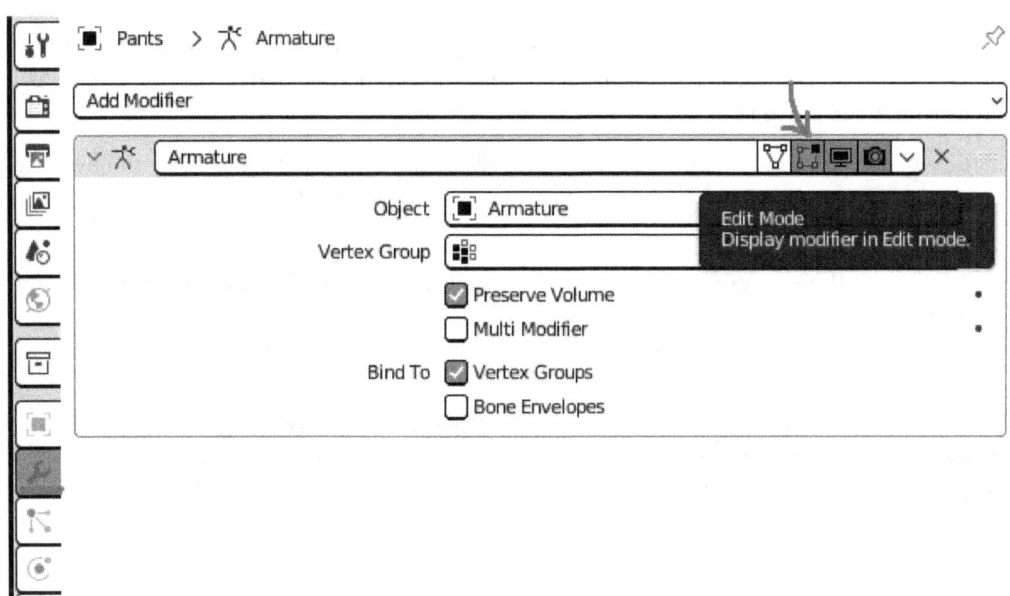

Figure 7.3 – Showing Armature deform modifier in Edit Mode

2. You should also enable the **Apply shape key in the edit mode** button for any shape keys you are working on. This is shown in *Figure 7.4*:

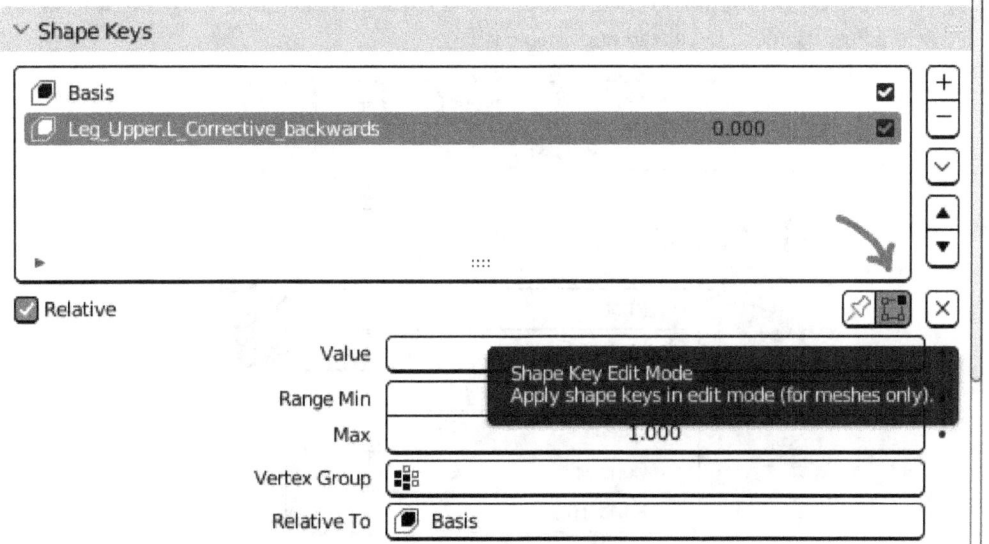

Figure 7.4 – Showing Armature deform modifier in Edit Mode

Do remember that this character is split into multiple meshes, each with its modifier and shape key sets, so as you progress you will need to enable **show in Edit Mode** on each mesh for any modifiers and shape keys.

3.   Because we are viewing this in Edit Mode, leaving the **Value** at **0** means we will never see anything, so move the **Value** slider up to **1**. Now we are editing the maximum value or 100% of the target shape.

That covers the Viewport tricks you need to make. Now let's go into **Edit Mode** to edit our new shape key.

> **Important note**
>
> Make sure you have the correct shape key selected. Please do not select the wrong one because it might take you hours to realize your mistake, and you will have to work through the shape creation process all over again.

Your character should still be in the pose shown in *Figure 7.1*. With the correct shape key selected, we will move the vertices into a shape that fixes the deformation issue. There are some tools we can use to make this quick – instead of selecting each vertex individually, there is Proportional Editing. **Proportional Editing** is a way of transforming selected elements while also affecting the nearby unselected elements. This is great as we can simply select one vertex and move the whole glute into shape.

4.   *Figure 7.5* shows the button to enable Proportional Editing and all the different modes you can use to adjust its effect. Go ahead and enable it.

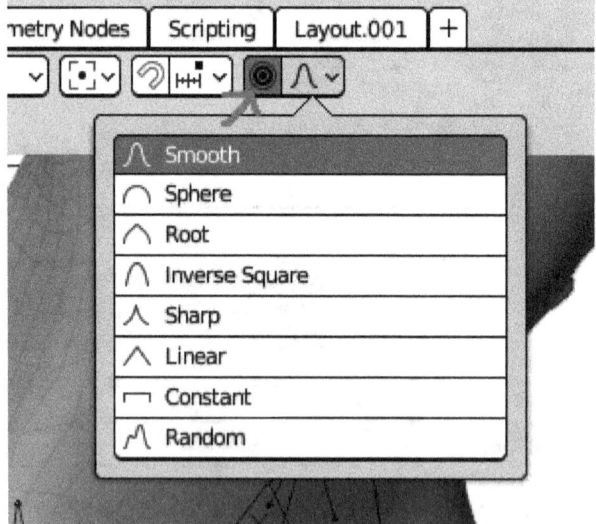

Figure 7.5 – Showing Armature deform modifier in Edit Mode

5. With Proportional Editing enabled, go into a side view and select a vertex that you think will be the center of the glute once pulled out. Press *G* to grab and pull this vertex into a position that gives you the desired shape but do not press any mouse buttons to confirm.

6. The Proportional Editing mode has a radius of effect that can be controlled with the mouse wheel. Scrolling up will increase the area and bring more vertices into effect while scrolling down will reduce the area of effect. Go ahead and adjust this as seen in the following screenshot:

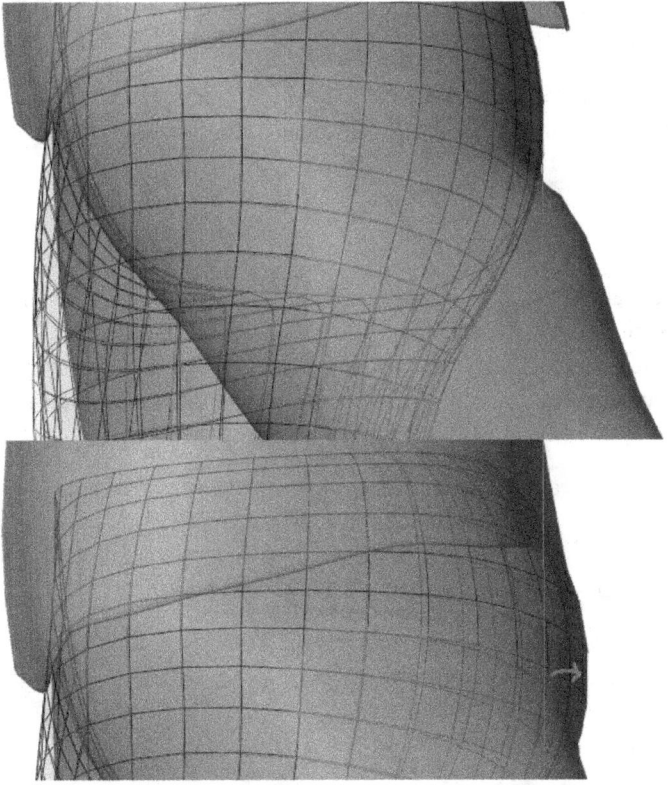

Figure 7.6 – Showing Armature deform modifier in Edit Mode

The top image in *Figure 7.6* shows the uncorrected mesh. The lower image shows the correction I have made. The red line through both images serves as a reference point for you to see how far out I have made my adjustments. Also note the shape I have given the adjusted shape key in the second half of the image.

With proportional editing still active, select a vertex that is in the middle and simply pull the glute out to your desired position. Use the scroll wheel to adjust the radius of the proportional editing

Once done, head back into **Object Mode** and have a little play with your new shape key. When you made the shape key in *Figure 7.4*, there was a **Value** slider. Go ahead and slide it around and watch how your shape key appears and disappears on the mesh.

Now you have a corrective shape key, wouldn't it be great if it could automatically appear and disappear as the leg bone swings backward and forward? We can do that with something called **drivers**. While you can use **Sculpt Mode**, we will not discuss it as it is out of scope for this topic. It is however advisable that you look into it as it will be of great use to you in both shape keys and general character creation/ modification.

So far, we have discussed shape keys and base keys, covering how to add both types, how to rename them, and how to edit each shape key with Edit Mode. In the next section, we will learn how to make these shape keys automatic. As they stand now, they can be animated manually using the **Value** slider.

We will finish this chapter by making Bone Drivers. These drivers may prove to be the most challenging part of this book but just stick with it. Once you understand how these drivers work you can use them anywhere you wish (Quite literally anywhere in Blender).

Using drivers

Drivers within Blender allow you to **drive any input field** with external numbers from other objects in the scene. In our case, we want to drive that **Value** slider for the shape key with the **rotation of the thigh** so that as we pull the leg back, its rotation drives the value of the shape key, making the process of applying shape keys automatic for any animators. If this wasn't the case animators would have to go through each shape key and manually add keyframes for their values.

This section will cover the creation of drivers, moving through each menu and popup to dig up this well-hidden Blender feature. Then we will move on to setting up the input of these drivers, choosing what bone we want to use to interact with this driver. By setting up the input, we will also set up the output – what we want this driver to do, which is drive a shape key!

We will finish with the complex task of adjusting this driver by using the **Driver Editor**, a neat tool that lets us visualize the relation between input and output.

Creating a driver

We first need to add a driver to the shape key. To do that, follow these steps:

1. Right-click the **Value** slider, which brings up a menu simply called **Value**.

2. Select **Add Driver** to add a driver and bring up its respective **Driven Property** menu, being careful to not move outside this new menu as it closes automatically when you move away from it.

3. If you happen to close this menu before finishing or wish to edit a driver you already made, there is an option called **Open Drivers Editor** in the same **Value** menu from *step 1*.

   Whether you are using the first **Driven Property** popup menu or the **Drivers Editor** window after choosing **Open Drivers Editor**, they both share the same basic controls so the following will apply to either. I will use the first menu for simplicity.

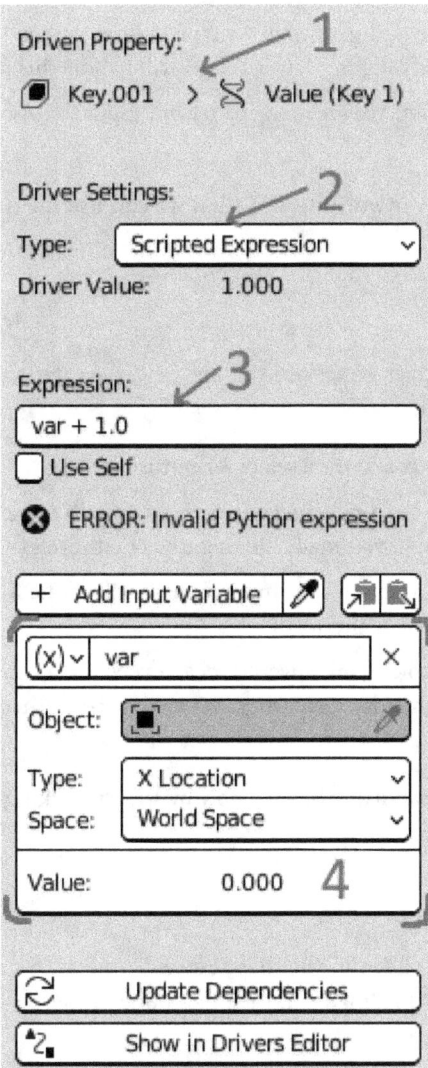

Figure 7.7 – Driven Property menu

It may seem to be very daunting but in reality, it's exceptionally simple after a couple of uses. I shall explain each important element in order (the following numbers refer to the preceding screenshot):

1. This shows both the current shape key we are driving and the specific driver we are editing. One shape key can have multiple drivers.

2. This determines the type of driver, essentially asking "What kind of input and what do we do with it?" We leave this on **Scripted Expression** for now. This allows us to adjust the input with some math, giving us better control over the end result.

3. The expression used. Depending on what we type in here, we can take the input of this driver and mathematically modify it. The Driver Editor will handle this for us

4. This whole box is our input. We are going to set our input to the back-and-forth swinging of the thigh.

We're first going to get this driver working and then we can use the driver editor to modify the sensitivity of the input.

Driver setup

All we need to do is feed this driver some value, in our case, the rotation of the hip. Inside box **4** of *Figure 7.7* is where we do just that:

1. Firstly, select the object box and then select **Armature**.
2. After doing this, you will see a **new box appear** underneath for selecting a specific bone. Set this box to the **thigh bone** (if you made the shape key on the left leg, then select the left thigh).
3. Set the type to the correct rotation axis. In our case, it will be the **X Rotation axis** as that is the axis the leg uses to swing back and forth.
4. Set **Space** to **Local**. If set to **Global**, it would mean even with a straight leg, rotating the whole armature would activate the shape key when we are only concerned about the rotation relative to the spine.

With that done, you can close that dialog box for now by simply clicking out of it. This will save the settings automatically.

Testing the driver

With the driver done, the **Value** slider for the shape key will now be in a new color. It may also have some arbitrary value because it's reading from the thigh bone as we speak. To test the driver, follow these steps:

1. Enter **Pose Mode** on the armature.
2. Move the thigh forward.
3. Leave **Pose Mode**.
4. Check the shape key value

Rotating the leg should change the value of the driver. When the driver is set up it might not start at 0 or go to 1, as long as the value changes that's what tells us we have made a working driver.

Adjusting drivers

Now you will undoubtedly have an issue here. You pulled the leg backward as far as you think is reasonable, but that value slider didn't move to **1.0** – it looks like the driver isn't strong enough, right? We can change how drivers behave in two ways: the Drivers Editor or by using Python.

I recommend the Drivers Editor as it's much easier to understand what's going on and it's a very visual method. Python on the other hand gives experts the chance to make magic and use far more complex tricks with multiple inputs. I will cover the Drivers Editor as that's what I recommend you stick to.

Drivers Editor

Editing drivers is the most complex task you will tackle in this book, but give it some patience and it will become routine.

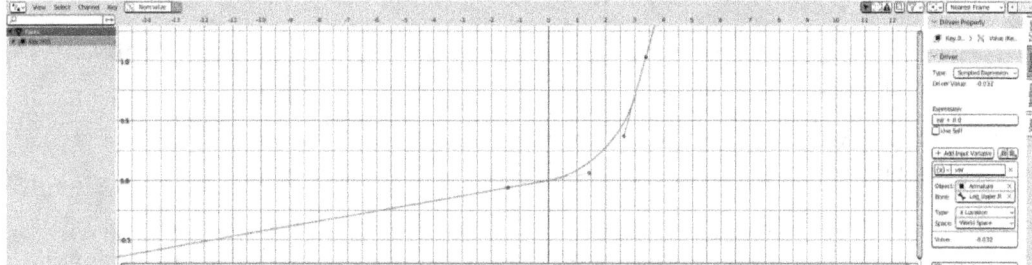

Figure 7.8 – An overview of the Drivers Editor window

The Drivers Editor is the best way to edit drivers as it shows the relation between input and output in a visual form and helps abstract all the complex Python math.

Using the dropdown in the top left of an area lets you change the editor type, just the same way as you have been changing between Object, Edit, and Pose Mode. Set the bottom area to **Drivers** and you will get to the window shown in *Figure 7.8*.

The left-hand axis shows the final output while the top axis represents the input. Editing this curve will change how the input affects the output.

With the **Drivers Editor** window open, select the shape key you wish to edit. On the left of the Drivers Editor, you can see the currently selected shape key and all the drivers under it. A shape key can have multiple drivers taking a wide range of inputs.

Its use is simple: by default, two points form the curve. Each point when selected will reveal a further two points on either side, These points are called handles, and the center point is simply referred to as the point. The center point controls the location of the point, and the outer handles control how the curve transitions from one point to another. These points are also shown in *Figure 7.8*, with two black spots (handles) flanking a center white spot (we are using the white theme, but your Blender instance may show different colors). Simply select any of the points and press *G* to move them. The effect will be immediately obvious as the curve will alter its shape.

There is a third point on the curve that becomes visible when the curve is selected. This third point shows where the current input is on the curve and its respective output. If you push a pose to its limits and know you want a specific readout, you can use this point to see where the readout is and adjust the curve to move this point where you want. Pressing *V* while selecting a point on the curve will bring up the **Set keyframe Handle type**. Each type changes how the two flanking handles behave. You shouldn't need to adjust this but it's there for any extreme cases.

One thing to note here is that the Drivers Editor is built from the F-Curve editor used in animation, which leads to a lot of animation-specific options being visible in the Drivers Editor. Some tools (such as the handle type) carry over in a useable form but most of the tools are useless, or confined to a very specific use. Essentially, if you are familiar with the F-Curve editor then you might be able to carry some tricks over from it, but if not then there's no need to worry.

If you don't know where to start, push the rig into a pose and move a point on the curve until you get your result. From there, keep tweaking.

This process is very visual and hands-on – experimenting with the driver curve is the best way you can learn about it.

Once you feel you finally have a good shape key, you'll now want to mirror it onto the other side – thankfully, you won't need to remake the whole shape key. We will cover mirroring shape keys next.

Mirroring shape keys

After all that work on the shape key, we don't want to have to do the same on the other side manually as that would take up a lot of time and would be asymmetrical. Thankfully, Blender lets us **mirror shape keys**. The following steps show how to mirror a shape key:

1. Select the shape key you wish to mirror and ensure its value is currently **1**, either by moving the slider or by posing any bones that drive the shape key. Make sure any other shape keys are **0** (you can simply delete drivers by right-clicking the **Value** slider).

2. Click the dropdown in *Figure 7.9* (marked **2**) to bring up the options for the currently selected shape key.

3. Use **New Shape from Mix** to create a new shape key that is a mix of the currently active shape keys. You can make a mix from an infinite amount of shape keys, but for now, we will use **Basis** and the shape key you wish to mirror.

4. Select this new shape key, go to the dropdown again, and use **the Mirror Shape key**. Note that there is also a **Mirror Shape Key (Topology)**, but let's ignore that as it's a very technical feature.

These steps are highlighted in the following screenshot:

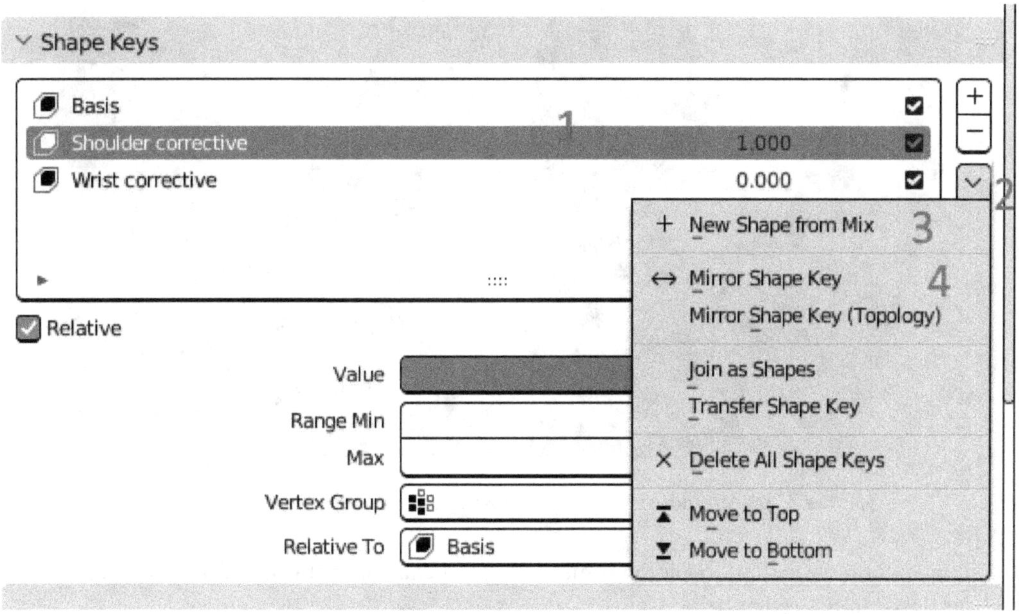

Figure 7.9 – Shape key options

What we just did was to make a duplicate shape key, and then we flipped it onto the other side. You will still have to set up the drivers again, but at least you saved time making the shape keys.

More shape key ideas

With that done, you have your first corrective shape key! As you have been stressing the model and revealing areas of poor deformation, you will have noticed that there are a few other spots that could do with some shape key help.

The following screenshots show the before and after results of the key areas that you can use shape keys to improve. We have already discussed all you need to know to replicate these, so you can go ahead and make some shape keys of your own. Maybe you can even find some other areas on your own in need of shape keys.

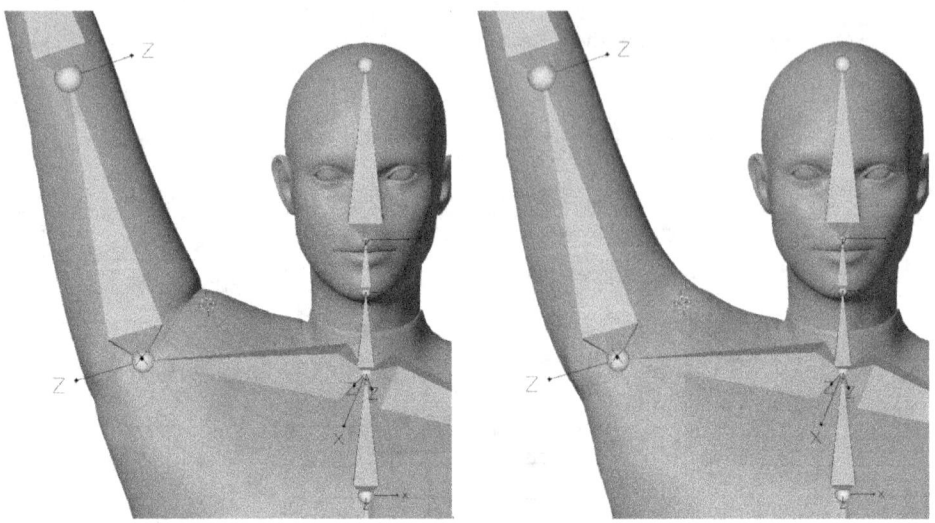

Figure 7.10 – Shoulder shape key removing the crease in the shoulder

From fixing poor deformation to adding some cloth-like behavior to the top of the shoulder, shape keys have near-limitless potential.

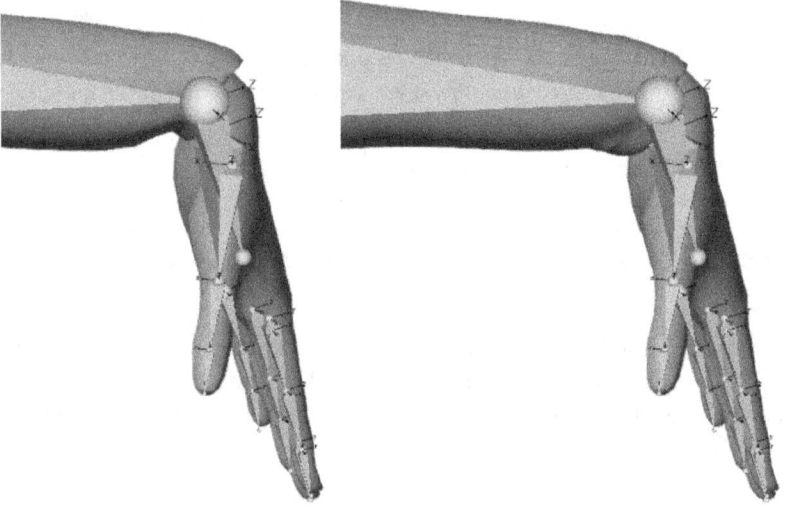

Figure 7.11 – Shape key fixing sleeve on the wrist

Creases such as that shown in the wrist in the preceding figure are some of the most common places to use shape keys, along with muscles and faces.

Sadly, you need to set up new drivers for each mirrored shape key as the drivers don't get mirrored over.

Summary

In this chapter, we have covered the use of both shape keys and drivers to *modify geometry automatically with bone input*. Understanding how drivers work and the importance of taking steps in the correct order will minimize time lost through error. We started the chapter by covering the creation of shape keys, remembering that you can use Sculpt Mode to make shape keys much faster (so you should go learn some sculpting!). We then moved on to the creation of drivers and the *Driver Editor* that can be used to modify these drivers. We finished the chapter by *mirroring the shape keys* to reduce our workload and *ensure symmetry*.

Before moving on to the next chapter, use the examples in *Figure 7.10* and *Figure 7.11* to practice and make more shape keys and drivers to improve areas of poor deformation. You will undoubtedly find more areas that could use the magic of shape keys, so don't be afraid to experiment!

In the final chapter, we will cover more advanced rigging ideas to give you an idea of where to go next in your learning. It's a chapter that requires no direct engagement, simply showing a collection of neat tips and tricks to improve your skills.

8

Beyond the Basics

By now, you should have all the knowledge needed to make basic rigs – from preparing the mesh, adding bones, and weight painting to custom handles and shape keys. This book has covered the very basics of rigging, while shape keys, constraints, and custom handles hint toward further development.

This chapter will touch on the further development of your rigging skills, showing what's possible with more advanced techniques. These examples will not contain explicit instructions but just the bare-bones information you need to replicate them. If you see something you like but can't figure out how to replicate it, then the final rig with these features will be made available for you to take a look at. If it's not on the rig, then a quick Google search will lead you to a guide, as rigging is well-documented online.

> **Important note**
>
> This chapter focuses on many constraints, and any constraint can and will interfere with other constraints and systems; sadly, that's just how Blender works. You can try changing the order of these systems by simply dragging the constraints to re-order them or using different constraints.

These examples are in no particular order to these topics. They serve as inspiration for you to expand your horizons in rigging and Blender.

This chapter aims to show you how complex rigging can become and all the creative ways you can achieve any goal. Understanding that there's always more out there that far surpasses what has been covered in this book and knowing that these skills exist will encourage you to push your envelope of understanding and lead to acquiring a deep skill set in rigging.

In this chapter, we will cover the following topics:

- Wrist bone twisting
- Topology in deformation
- Bendy bones
- Damped Track
- Add-ons to expand your toolbox

Wrist bone twisting

A very common problem you might have with the rig is the exceptionally poor deformation of the wrist. While this can be fixed with shape keys, you may find that you are not able to use shape keys due to other limitations (pipeline, game engine, render engine, export/import restrictions, and so on). *Figure 8.1* shows before and after adding a wrist twist:

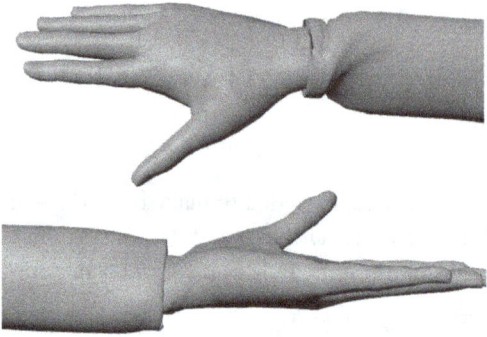

Figure 8.1 – Wrist twist

In *Figure 8.1*, you can see that the top hand has terrible deformation at the wrist, while the bottom hand spreads the twist out along the forearm, just as our arms do.

The next screenshot shows how the bones are set up and the constraints used:

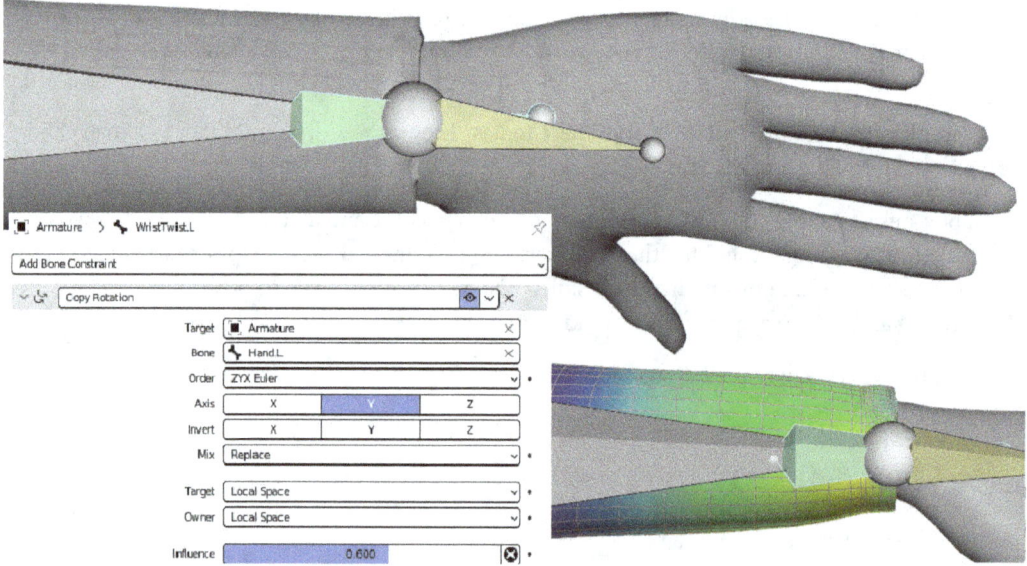

Figure 8.2 – Wrist twist setup

Let's look at this in more detail.

The yellow bone is the IK target. The green bone is a new bone used for the wrist twist setup.

The green bone is parented to the forearm, with a **Copy Rotation** constraint targeting the hand at a 0.600 influence. This makes the bone average the rotation between the forearm and hand.

The green bone has very light weights on the sleeve and the skin under it; when the bone twists, it will take the sleeve gently with it.

Topology in deformation

The topology of a model greatly affects its deformation. While this leans more toward modeling rather than rigging, it can be really helpful to know that there are ways of achieving better deformation that you might not have expected. *Figure 8.3* shows some good basic examples of how different topologies can affect the result of the deformation:

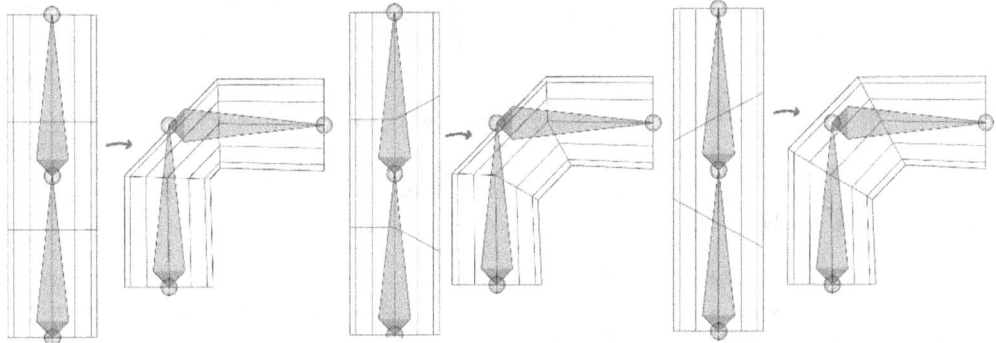

Figure 8.3 – Basic topology, deformation silhouettes

The next screenshot, *Figure 8.4*, shows a potential solution to achieve decent deformation on a bend:

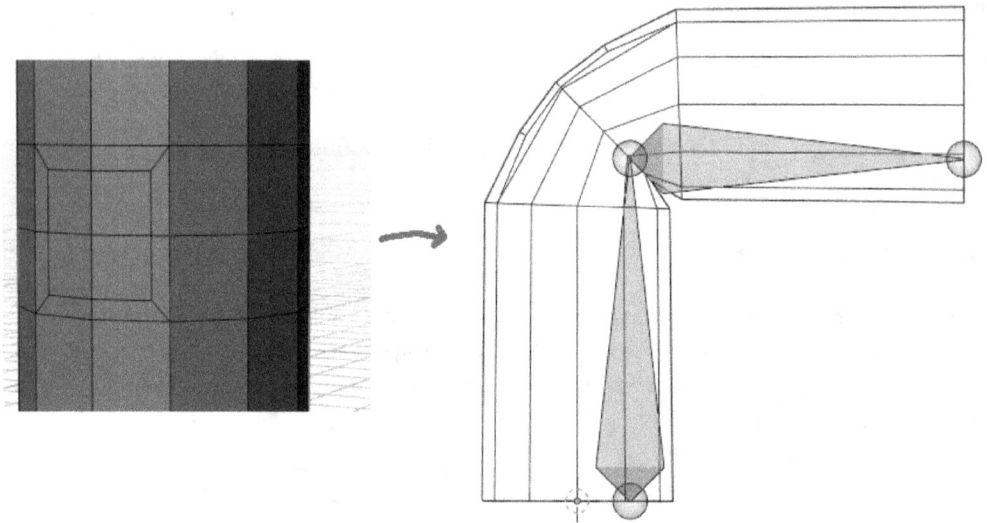

Figure 8.4 – Common topology for bends

You can mix these examples (and many other ideas) to combine their effects, and an experienced artist can integrate these basic principles into a dense and complex model.

Sore spots such as elbows and knees are prime contenders for topology bends, but you need to be expecting issues in advance of making the character because it affects the way the model needs to be made. The model provided did not include any of these as it wasn't necessary.

Bendy bones

Blender has two types of bones: *normal* and *bendy*. In this book you have been using normal bones because there has been no need to use anything else. Bendy bones are great for making whacky and wild rigs, most typically found in lighthearted animated films where the characters do not conform to the logic of real life.

Figure 8.5 shows everything needed to turn a bone into a bendy bone; add some IK to the end handle and it's simple!

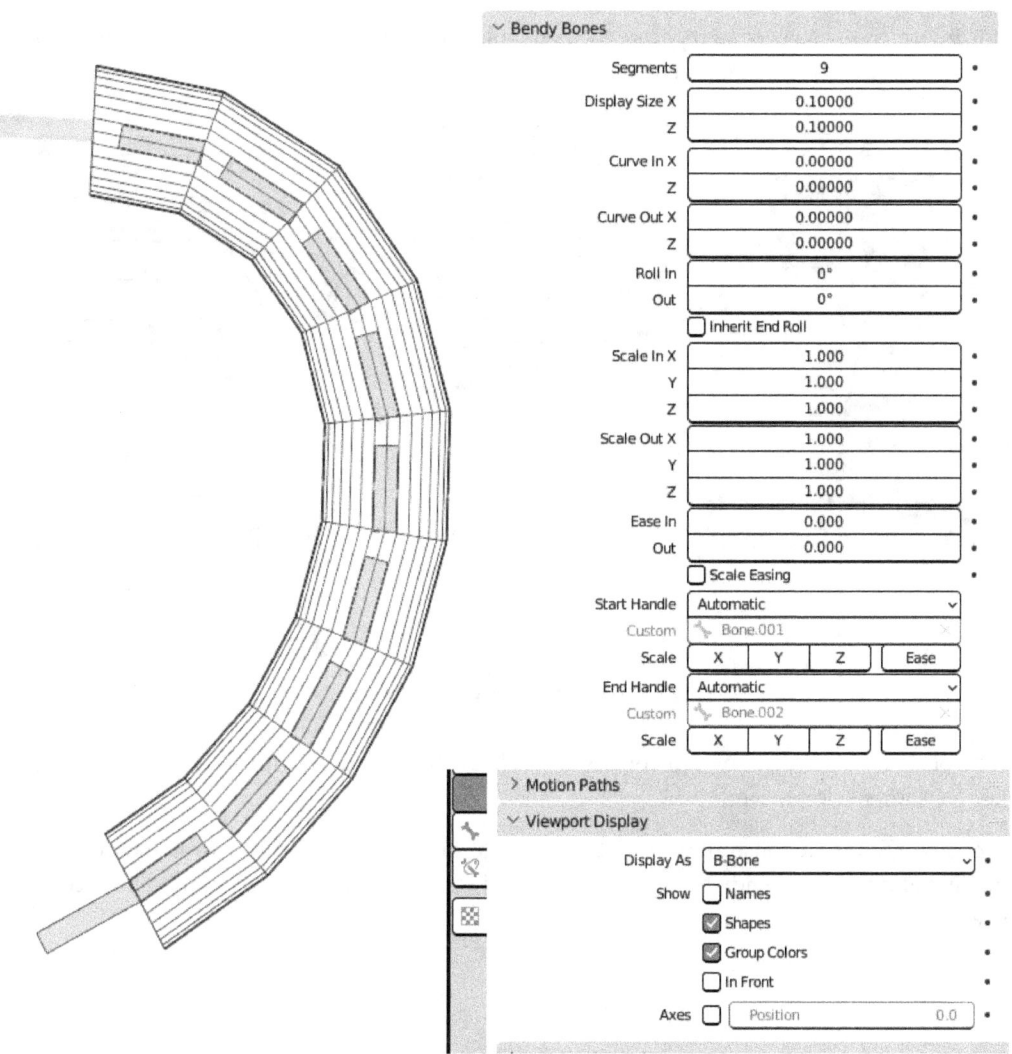

Figure 8.5 – Full bendy bone setup

All the information you need to replicate each example is in these figures, so should you ever need to come back for ideas, you can take a quick look.

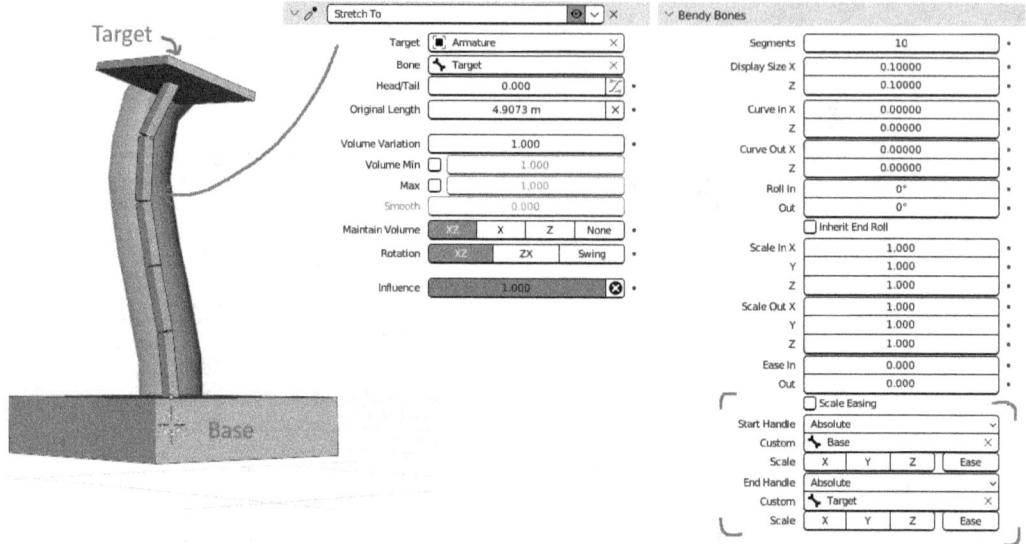

Figure 8.6 – Full bendy bone setup

A control rig for a bendy bone can consist of a **Stretch To** constraint with a disconnected target. *Figure 8.6* shows a simple setup.

There's also a **Spine** IK constraint; it's pretty similar to the other IK constraints you have used and comes in handy when a bendy bone is not supported by an export target or you need finer control over a chain of bones.

Damped Track

Damped Track is great for making one bone point toward another. I find placing a **Damped Track** constraint on the head is always a good idea; it's a simple constraint but an exceptionally effective one. *Figure 8.7* shows a **Damped Track** constraint in action:

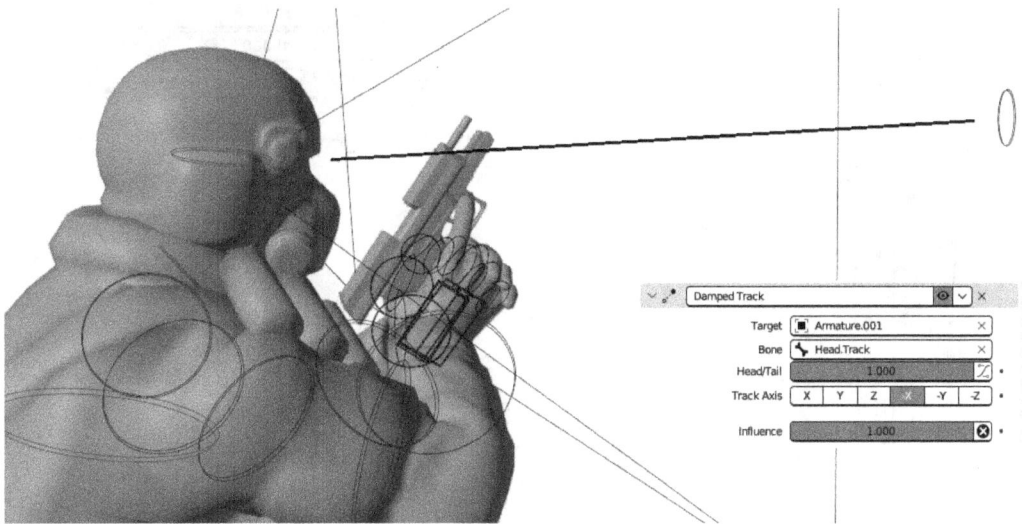

Figure 8.7 – Damped Track

Damped Track can be used for many different things, mostly when pointing at an object.

A surprise place you can use **Damped Track** is in a tail!

Model a simple tail and place a chain of bones in it. I used automatic weights just to keep it quick (great when it works).

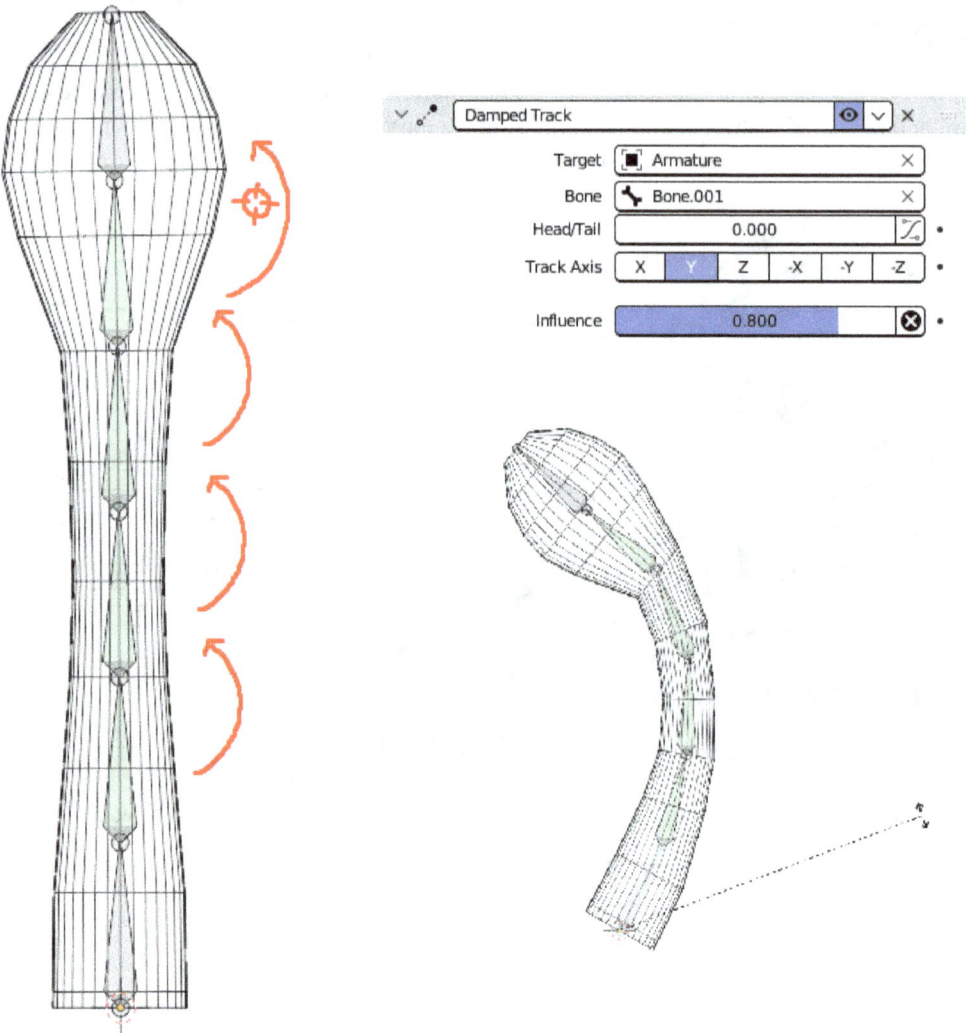

Figure 8.8 – Damped Track in a tail setup

Each bone in the chain has a **Damped Track** constraint that targets the bone above it; it's as simple as that, but grab the base bone and rotate it to see how impressively effective the result is! Note the **Influence** value; the stronger the value, the stronger the effect.

This lets you put the base bone on a simple loop and have the rest of the tail move behind automatically!

Add-ons to expand your toolbox

Everything discussed in this book has been part of the default Blender experience. While Blender manages to cover such impressive depths, add-ons can completely change how you approach rigging.

Admittedly, some of these add-ons may do you more harm than good (Auto-Rig add-ons come to mind), but there are a few that are genuinely great. A few personal favorites are as follows:

- **Wiggle Bones**: Assign a bone to be a wiggle bone, then animate any bones above it; this add-on gives set bones a nice touch of physics. It leans more toward animation but it's a fantastic tool to know about, just in case someone asks for a rig with little stringy things that need to jiggle (or not so stringy).

- **Bone Manager**: Assigning bone groups can be a little unsightly. All of those dots in the Layers grid just look daft, right? Bone Manager adds a new UI where you can name bone groups and even add scene controls to switch selected bone groups on the fly. Animators are always happy to see stuff like this!

- **Dynamic Parent**: Now, admittedly, this is an animator's tool. That doesn't mean you don't need to know about it. This add-on allows you to quickly enable/disable parent-child relationships between objects. This is done through the animated **Child** of Constraint. When disabled, the child's position relative to the parent is preserved. This goes for bones too.

There are so many more add-ons, including ones that neither you nor I know of! They have such great power that you should always be on the lookout for any to add to your tools.

Summary

This chapter has been all about expanding your newfound skills in rigging, from Blender's own included tools to add-ons that can change how you think about rigging. There are plenty of professional riggers out there who are sharing even more tips and tricks on the internet. Seeing what others are doing and how they go about their work is the best way for you to learn and grow in any skill, so make sure you are keeping your eyes peeled for anything rigging-related out there.

By this point, you have covered everything you need to know to give life to mesh – from the humble beginnings of an empty scene and working with mesh to adding armatures and then bones in Edit mode. You know about parenting mesh to bones and how that relationship works, using weights to bind vertices to bones. You furthered your skills by using the weight painting tools to precisely paint weights, adjusting both weights and bone positions while pushing your work into stress poses that show any shortcomings. You learned that success comes from repeated trial and error, and in that back-and-forth loop of iteration comes experience and instinct.

With this book finished, you now have the foundations you need to conquer more aspects of creative 3D work, creating an array of works you can use to impress people and secure yourself a spot in a creatively rewarding industry.

Index

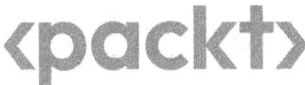

`Packtpub.com`

Subscribe to our online digital library for full access to over 7,000 books and videos, as well as industry leading tools to help you plan your personal development and advance your career. For more information, please visit our website.

Why subscribe?

- Spend less time learning and more time coding with practical eBooks and Videos from over 4,000 industry professionals

- Improve your learning with Skill Plans built especially for you

- Get a free eBook or video every month

- Fully searchable for easy access to vital information

- Copy and paste, print, and bookmark content

Did you know that Packt offers eBook versions of every book published, with PDF and ePub files available? You can upgrade to the eBook version at `packtpub.com` and as a print book customer, you are entitled to a discount on the eBook copy. Get in touch with us at `customercare@packtpub.com` for more details.

At `www.packtpub.com`, you can also read a collection of free technical articles, sign up for a range of free newsletters, and receive exclusive discounts and offers on Packt books and eBooks.

Other Books You May Enjoy

If you enjoyed this book, you may be interested in these other books by Packt:

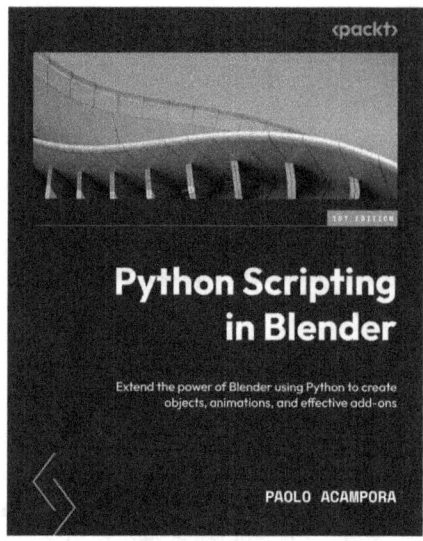

Python Scripting in Blender

Paolo Acampora

ISBN: 978-1-80323-422-9

- Understand the principles of 3D and programming and learn how they operate in Blender.
- Build engaging and navigation-friendly user interfaces that integrate with the native look and feel.
- Respect coding guidelines and deliver readable and compliant code without the loss of originality.
- Package your extensions into a complete add-on, ready for installation and distribution.

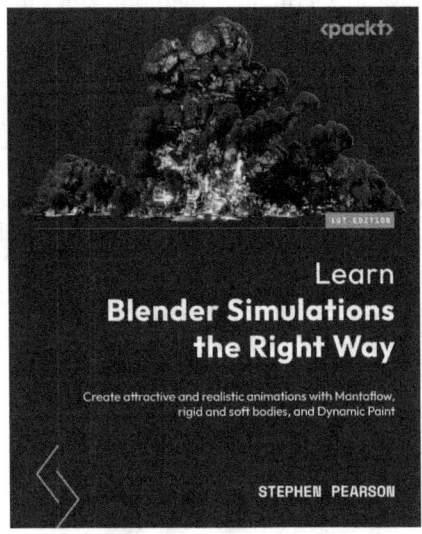

Learn Blender Simulations the Right Way

Stephen Pearson

ISBN: 978-1-80323-415-1

- Discover what Mantaflow is and how to use it effectively.
- Understand domains, flows, and effectors, and why they are important.
- Create realistic fire, smoke, and fluid simulations.
- Produce satisfying soft and rigid body simulations with ease.
- Use the cloth simulation to bring animated fabric to life.
- Explore canvas and brush objects in Dynamic Paint to create eye-catching animations.

Packt is searching for authors like you

If you're interested in becoming an author for Packt, please visit `authors.packtpub.com` and apply today. We have worked with thousands of developers and tech professionals, just like you, to help them share their insight with the global tech community. You can make a general application, apply for a specific hot topic that we are recruiting an author for, or submit your own idea.

Share Your Thoughts

Now you've finished *3D Character Rigging in Blender*, we'd love to hear your thoughts! Scan the QR code below to go straight to the Amazon review page for this book and share your feedback or leave a review on the site that you purchased it from.

`https://packt.link/r/1-803-23880-1`

Your review is important to us and the tech community and will help us make sure we're delivering excellent quality content.

Download a free PDF copy of this book

Thanks for purchasing this book!

Do you like to read on the go but are unable to carry your print books everywhere?

Is your eBook purchase not compatible with the device of your choice?

Don't worry, now with every Packt book you get a DRM-free PDF version of that book at no cost.

Read anywhere, any place, on any device. Search, copy, and paste code from your favorite technical books directly into your application.

The perks don't stop there, you can get exclusive access to discounts, newsletters, and great free content in your inbox daily

Follow these simple steps to get the benefits:

1. Scan the QR code or visit the link below

https://packt.link/free-ebook/978-1-80323-880-7

2. Submit your proof of purchase
3. That's it! We'll send your free PDF and other benefits to your email directly